Learn to Write the Alphabet -
All Toys

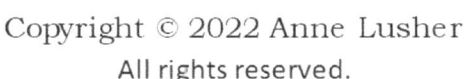

The Danger Twins
Writing Series

ISBN PAPERBACK: 978-1-956547-05-4

Book design by Anne Lusher
Published by Unplanned Books, LLC.

UNPLANNED BOOKS

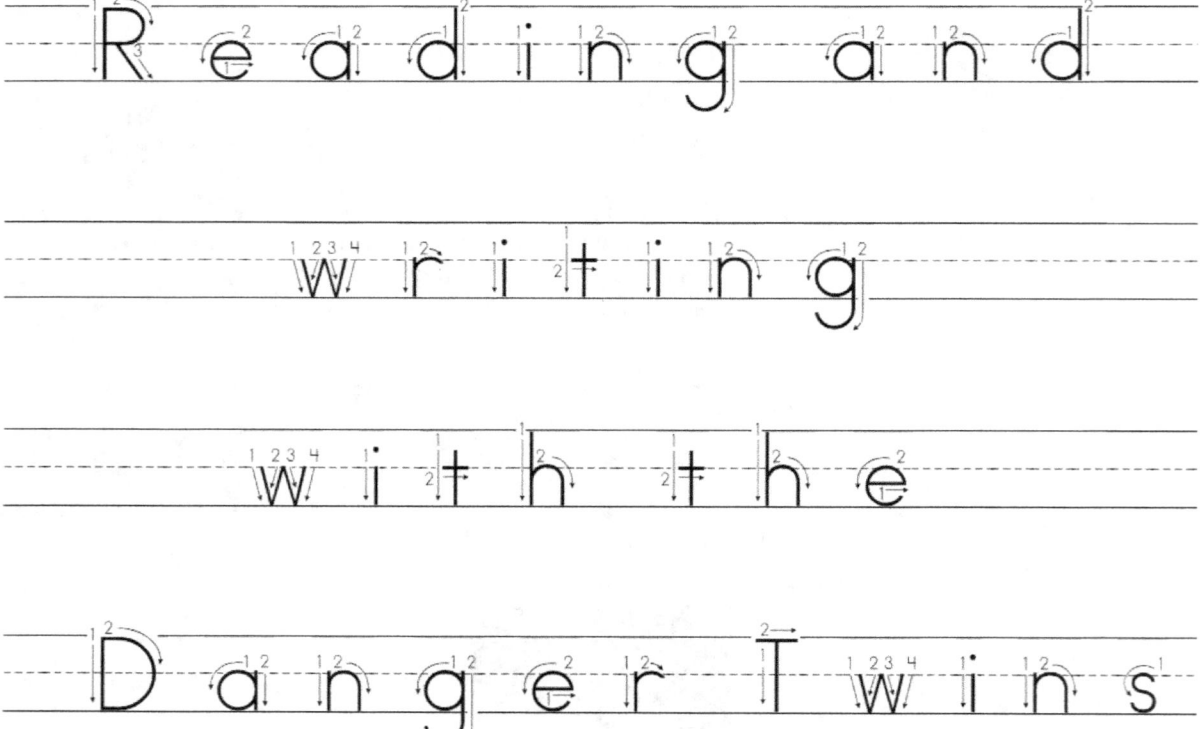

Reading and writing with the Danger Twins

WRITING WITH THE DANGER TWINS

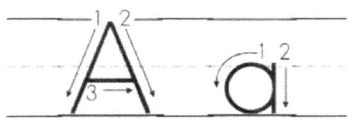 Trace the individual letters. Then trace each toy name and then say it aloud.

A A A A A A A

A A A A A A A

a a a a a a a

a b a c u s

a b a c u s

a b a c u s

a

WRITING WITH THE DANGER TWINS

B b

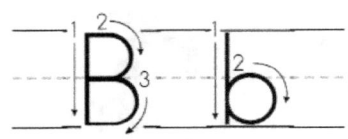

Trace the individual letters.
Then trace each toy name
and then say it aloud.

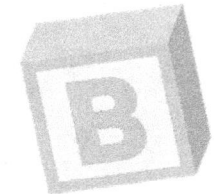

B B B B B B B

B B B B B B B

b b b b b b b

basketball

basketball

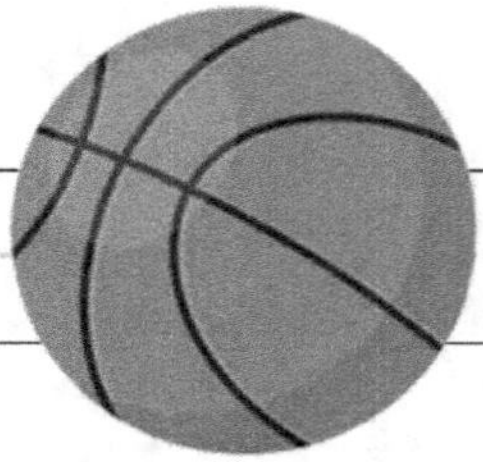

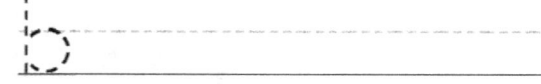

basketball

b

C c

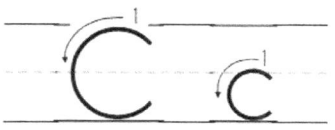

Trace the individual letters.
Then trace each toy name
and then say it aloud.

C C C C C C

C C C C C C

c c c c c c c

crayons

crayons

crayons

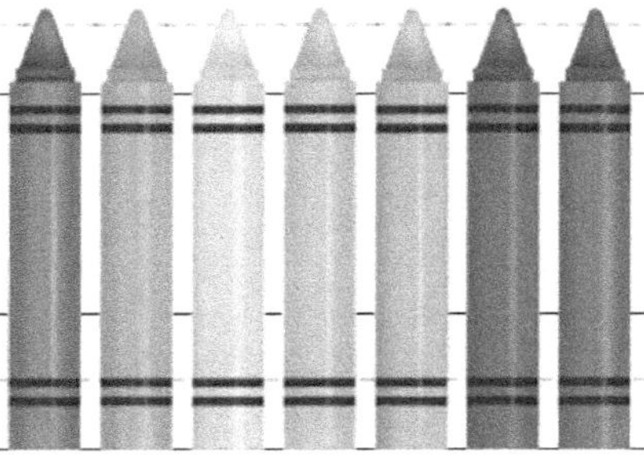

c

Dd

Trace the individual letters. Then trace each toy name and then say it aloud.

D

D D D D D D D

D D D D D D D

d d d d d d d

d r u m

d r u m

d r u m

d

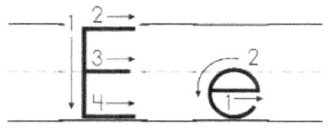

Trace the individual letters.
Then trace each toy name
and then say it aloud.

E E E E E E E

E E E E E E E

e e e e e e e

easel

easel

easel

e

WRITING WITH THE DANGER TWINS

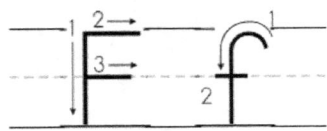

Trace the individual letters. Then trace each toy name and then say it aloud.

F F F F F F F

F F F F F F F

f f f f f f f

frisbee

frisbee

frisbee

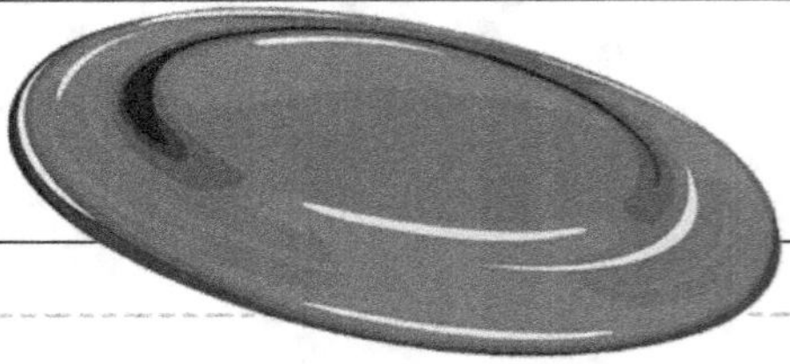

f

WRITING WITH THE DANGER TWINS

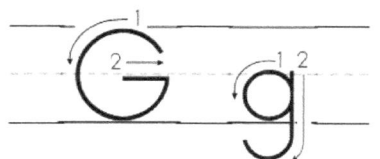 Trace the individual letters. Then trace each toy name and then say it aloud.

G G G G G G

G G G G G G

g g g g g g g g

guitar

guitar

guitar

g

WRITING WITH THE DANGER TWINS

Trace the individual letters. Then trace each toy name and then say it aloud.

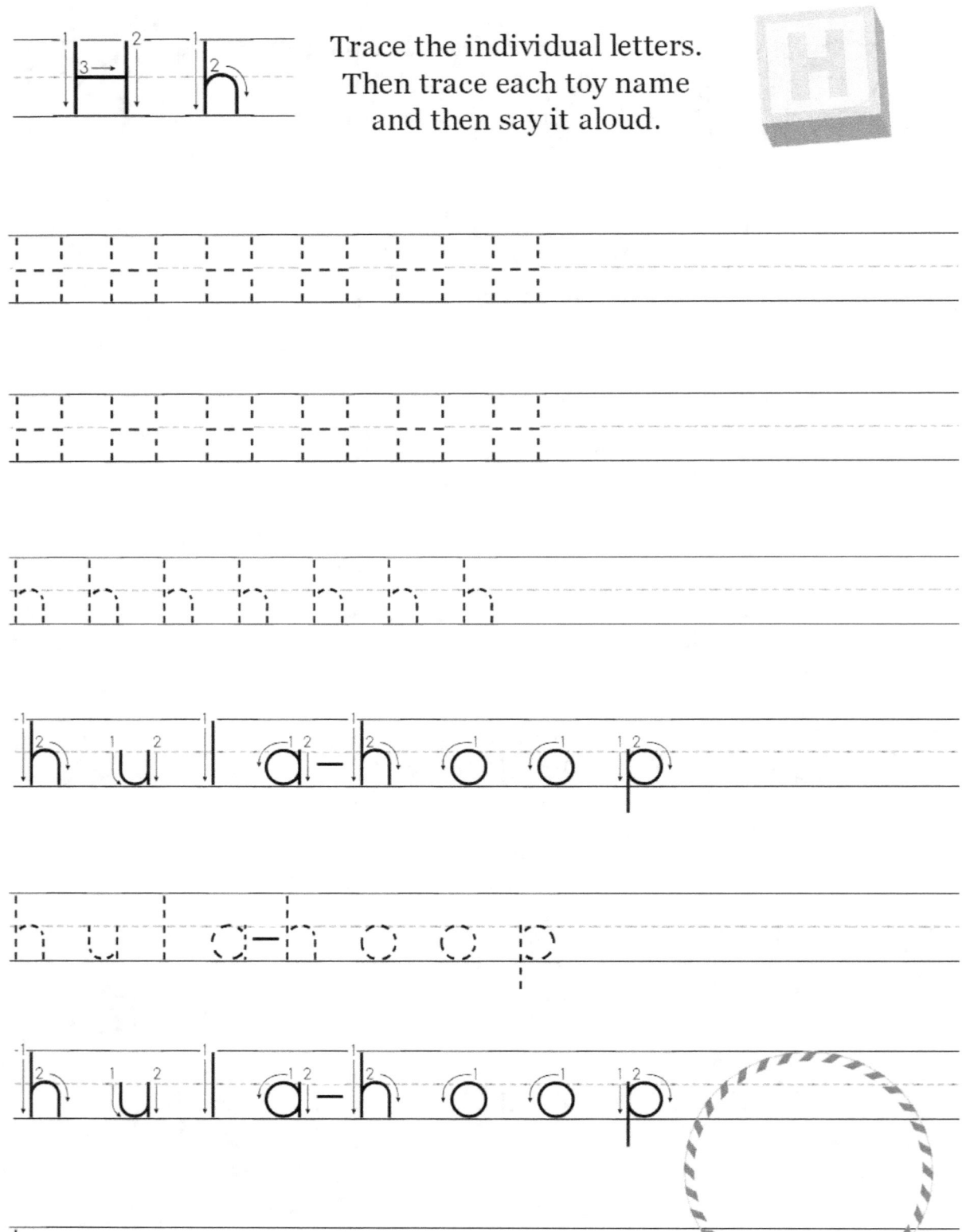

hhhhhh

h u l a - h o o p

h u l a - h o o p

h u l a - h o o p

Trace the individual letters.
Then trace each toy name
and then say it aloud.

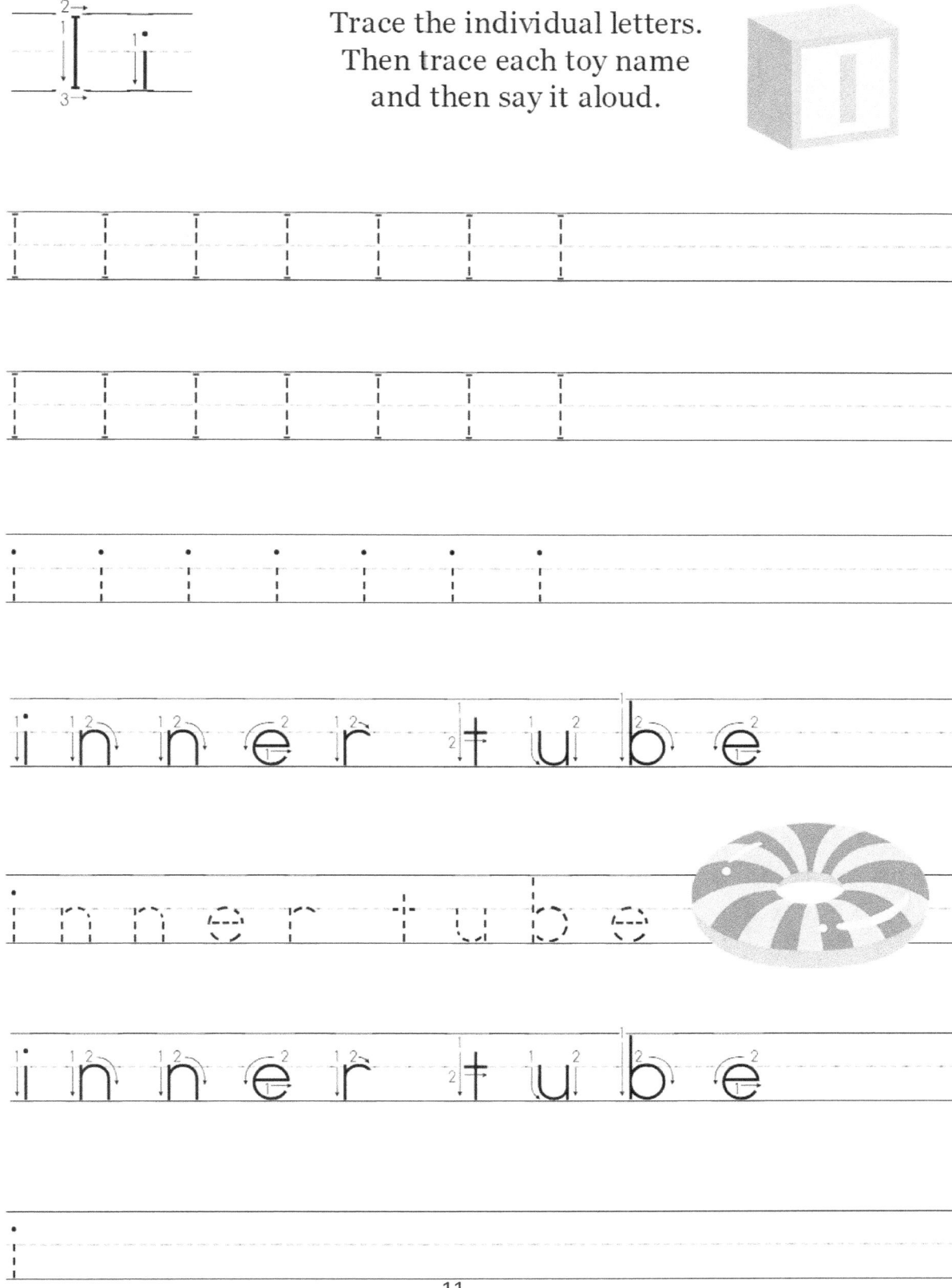

inner tube

inner tube

inner tube

WRITING WITH THE DANGER TWINS

J j

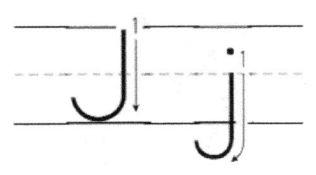

Trace the individual letters.
Then trace each toy name
and then say it aloud.

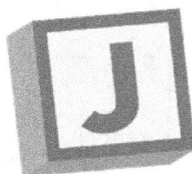

J J J J J J J

J J J J J J J

j j j j j j j j

jump rope

jump rope

jump rope

j

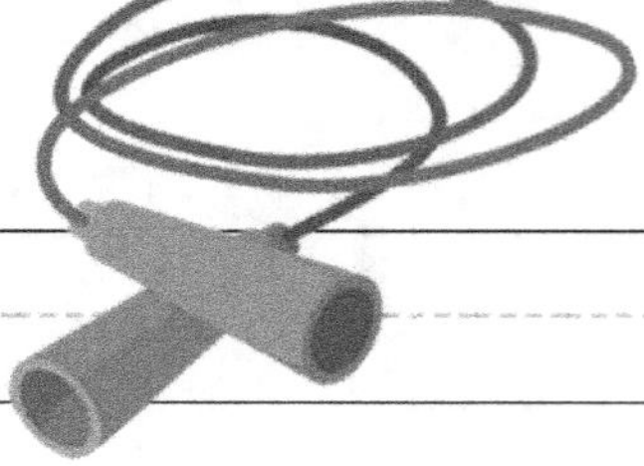

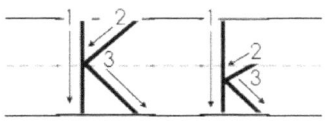

Trace the individual letters.
Then trace each toy name
and then say it aloud.

K K K K K K

K K K K K K

K K K K K K K

kite

kite

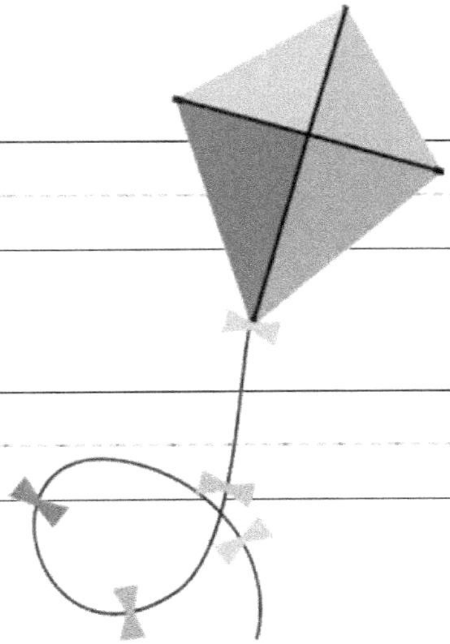

kite

k

WRITING WITH THE DANGER TWINS

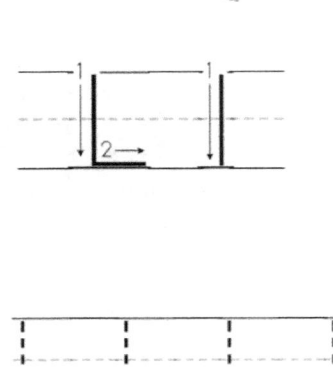

Trace the individual letters.
Then trace each toy name
and then say it aloud.

l o c k e t

o c k e t

l o c k e t

Trace the individual letters.
Then trace each toy name
and then say it aloud.

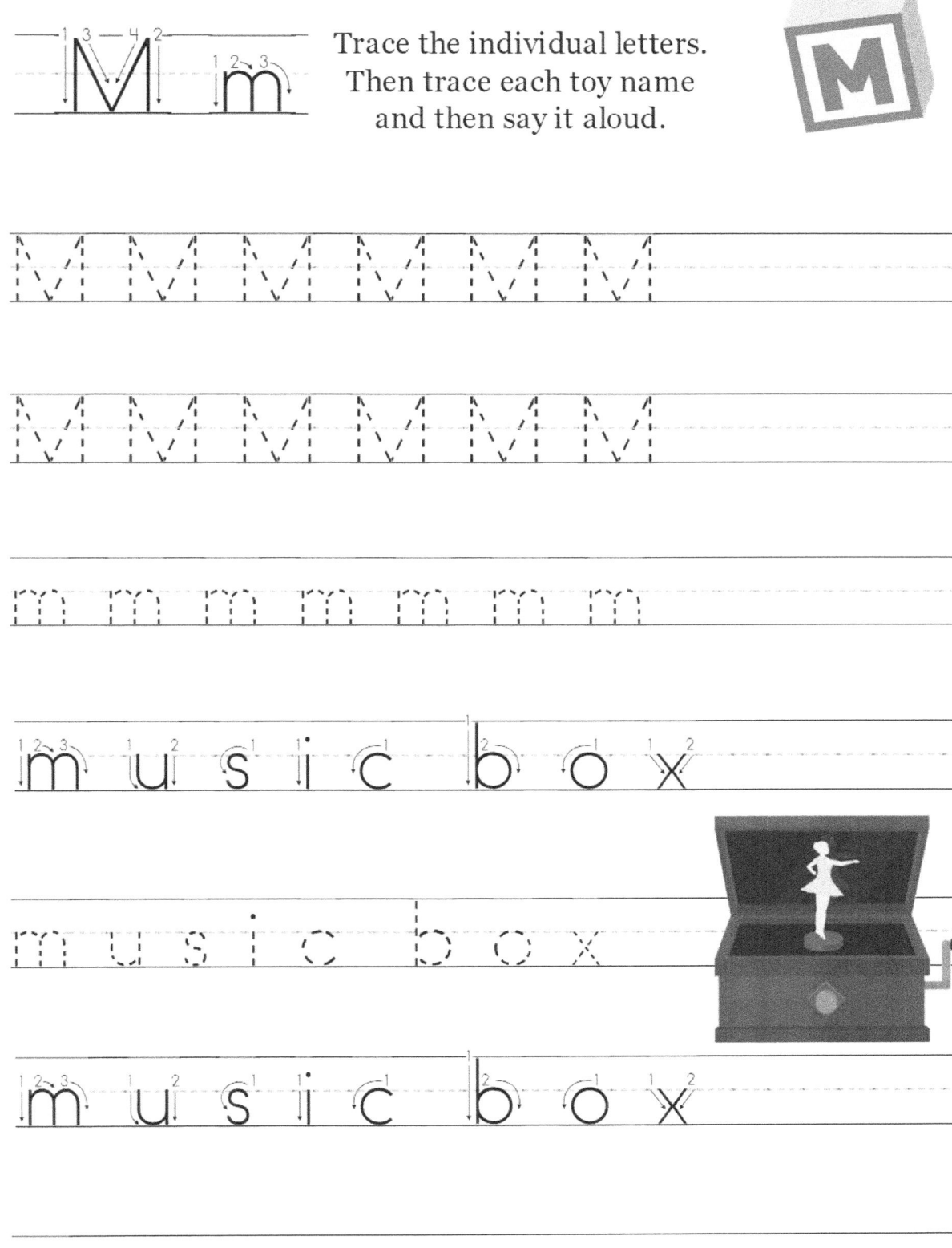

M M M M M M M

M M M M M M M

m m m m m m m

music box

music box

music box

m

Trace the individual letters.
Then trace each toy name
and then say it aloud.

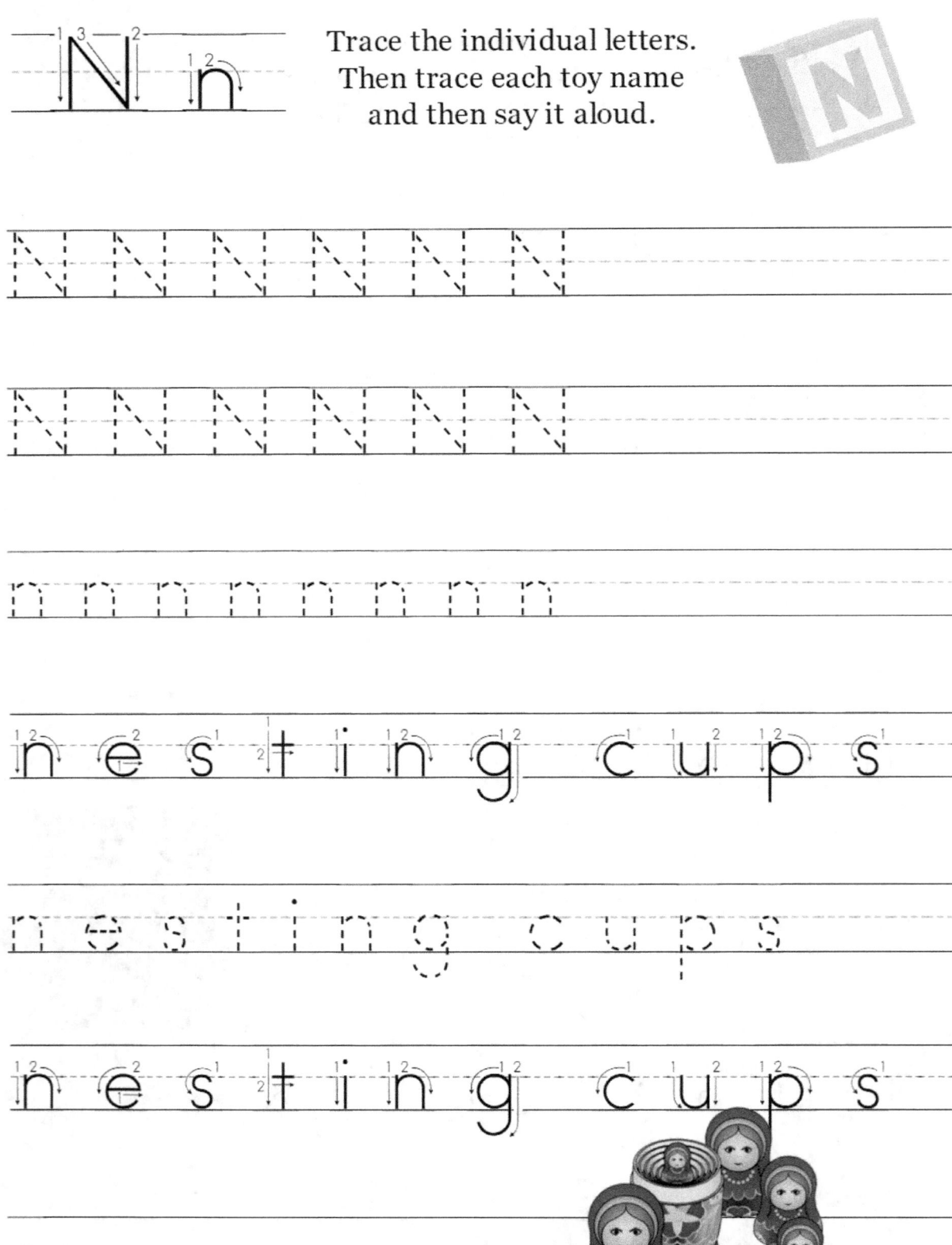

N N N N N N N

N N N N N N

n n n n n n n n

nesting cups

nesting cups

nesting cups

n

WRITING WITH THE DANGER TWINS

Trace the individual letters.
Then trace each toy name
and then say it aloud.

O O O O O O

O O O O O

o o o o o o o o

o v e n

o v e n

o v e n

o

WRITING WITH THE DANGER TWINS

Pp

Trace the individual letters. Then trace each toy name and then say it aloud.

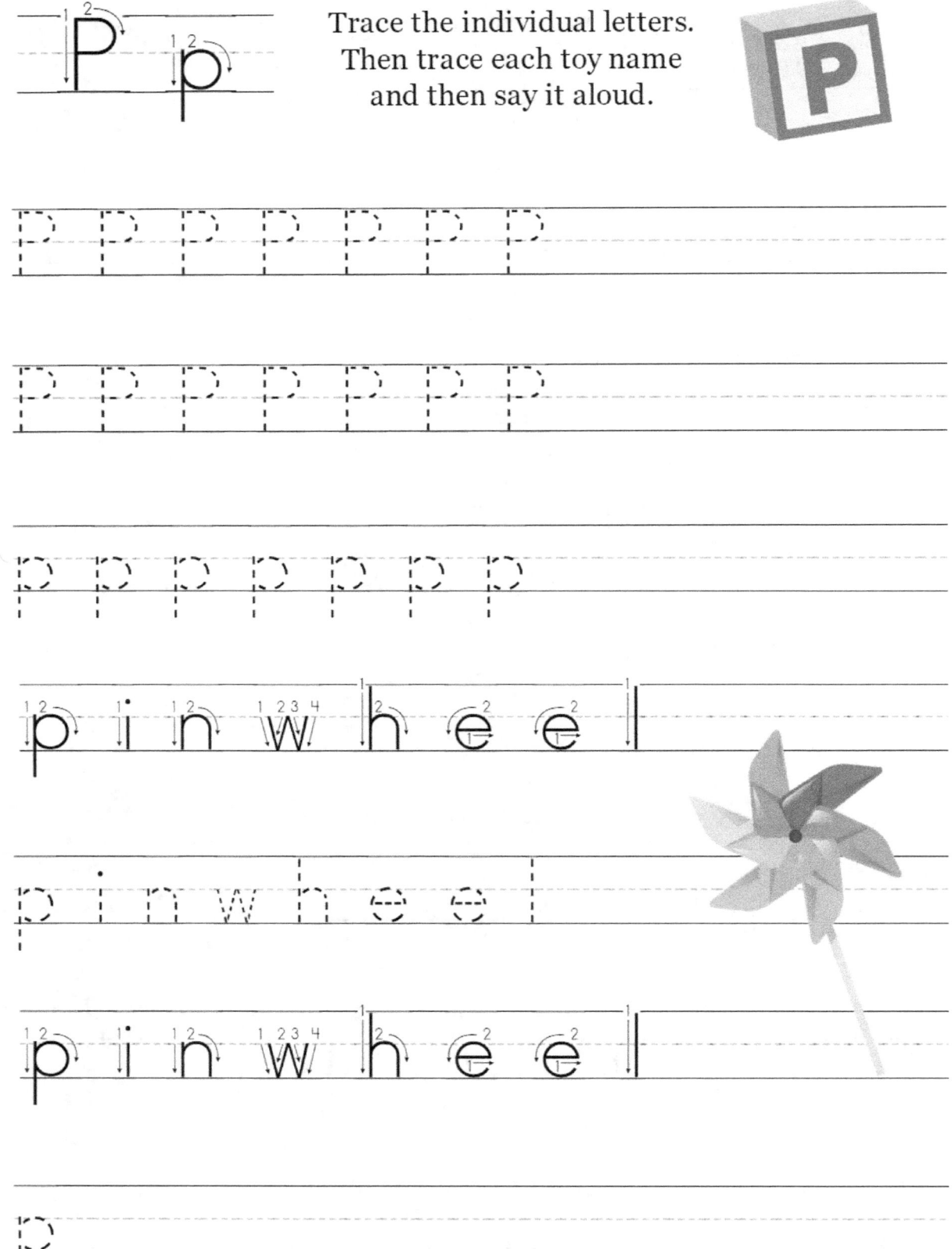

P P P P P P P

P P P P P P P

P P P P P P P

pinwheel

pinwheel

pinwheel

p

WRITING WITH THE DANGER TWINS

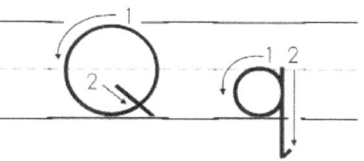

Trace the individual letters.
Then trace each toy name
and then say it aloud.

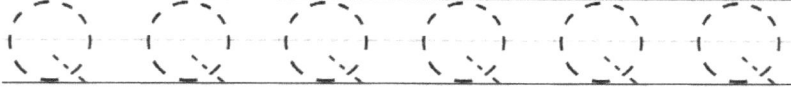

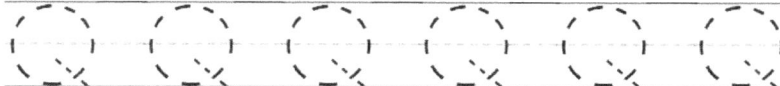

q q q q q q q

q u a d

q u a d

q u a d

q

WRITING WITH THE DANGER TWINS

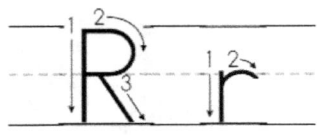

Trace the individual letters. Then trace each toy name and then say it aloud.

R R R R R R

R R R R R R

r r r r r r r

r o b o t

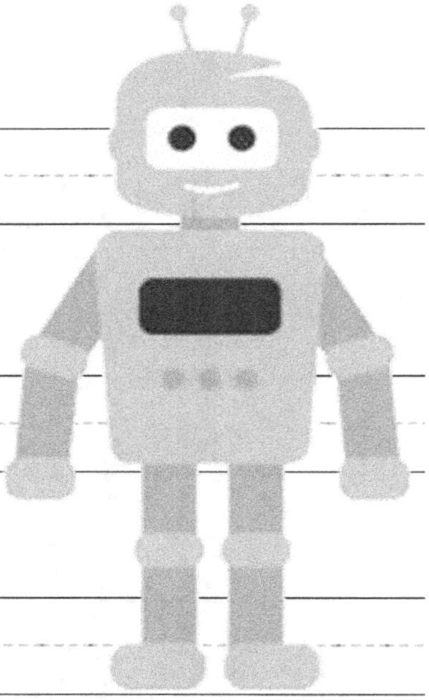

r o b o t

r o b o t

r

WRITING WITH THE DANGER TWINS

 Trace the individual letters.
Then trace each toy name
and then say it aloud.

S S S S S S

S S S S S S

s s s s s s s

s o c c e r   b a l l

s o c c e r   b a l l

s o c c e r   b a l l

s

WRITING WITH THE DANGER TWINS

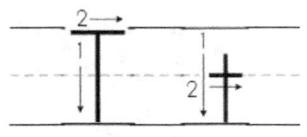

Trace the individual letters.
Then trace each toy name
and then say it aloud.

T T T T T

T T T T T

t t t t t t t t t

tricycle

tricycle

tricycle

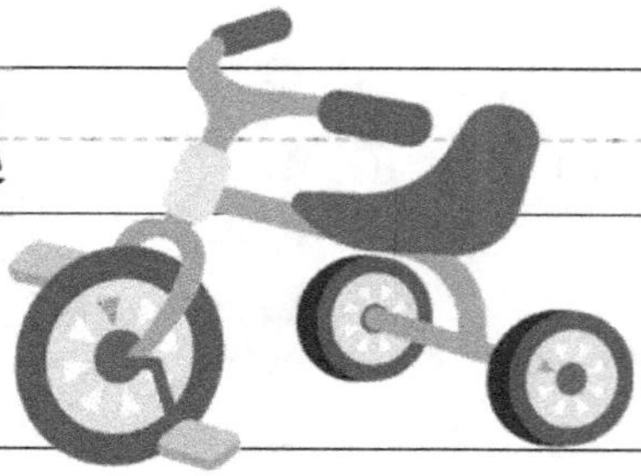

t

U u

Trace the individual letters.
Then trace each toy name
and then say it aloud.

U U U U U U

U U U U U U

U U U U U U U

u n i c y c l e

u n i c y c l e

u n i c y c l e

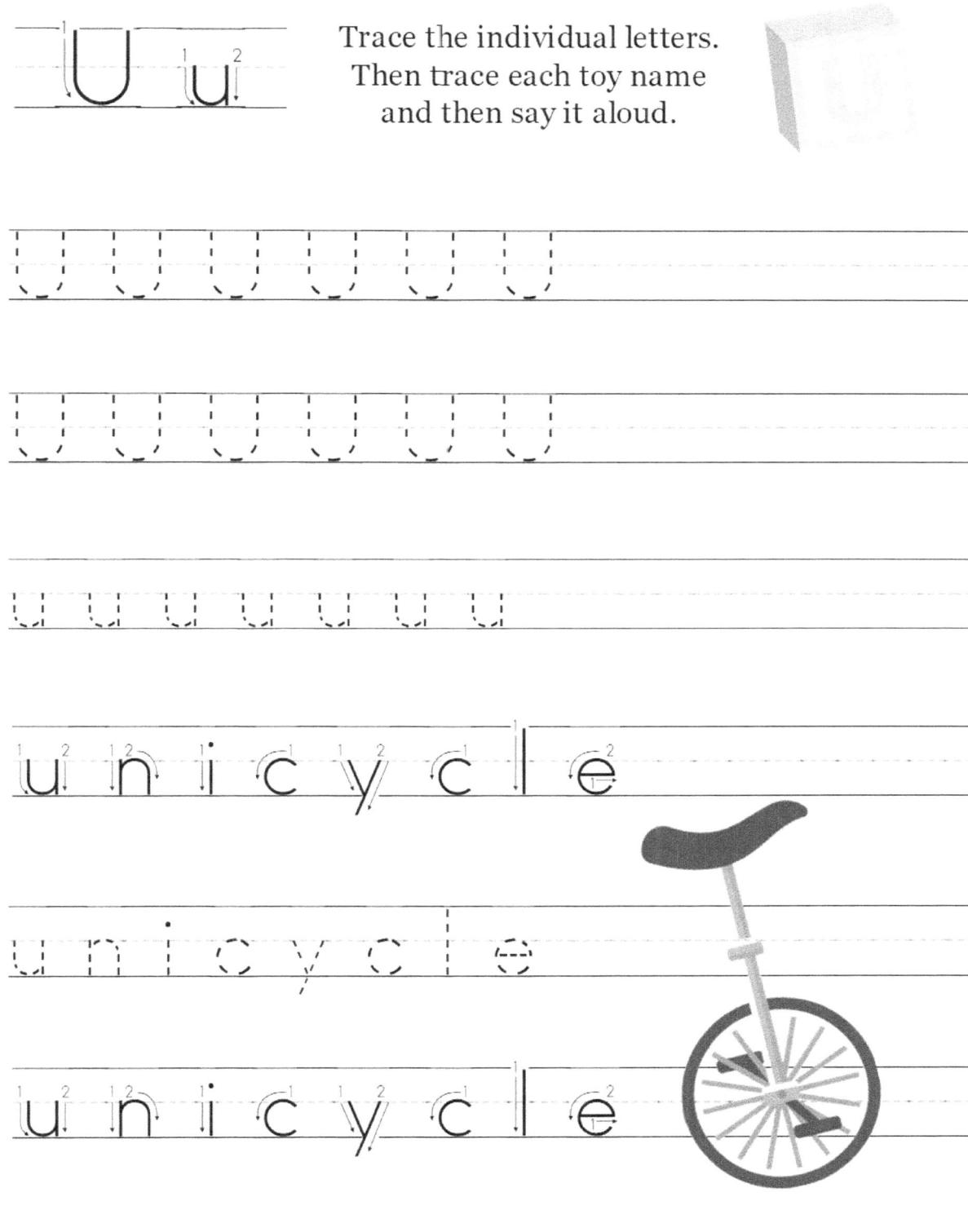

u

Trace the individual letters. Then trace each toy name and then say it aloud.

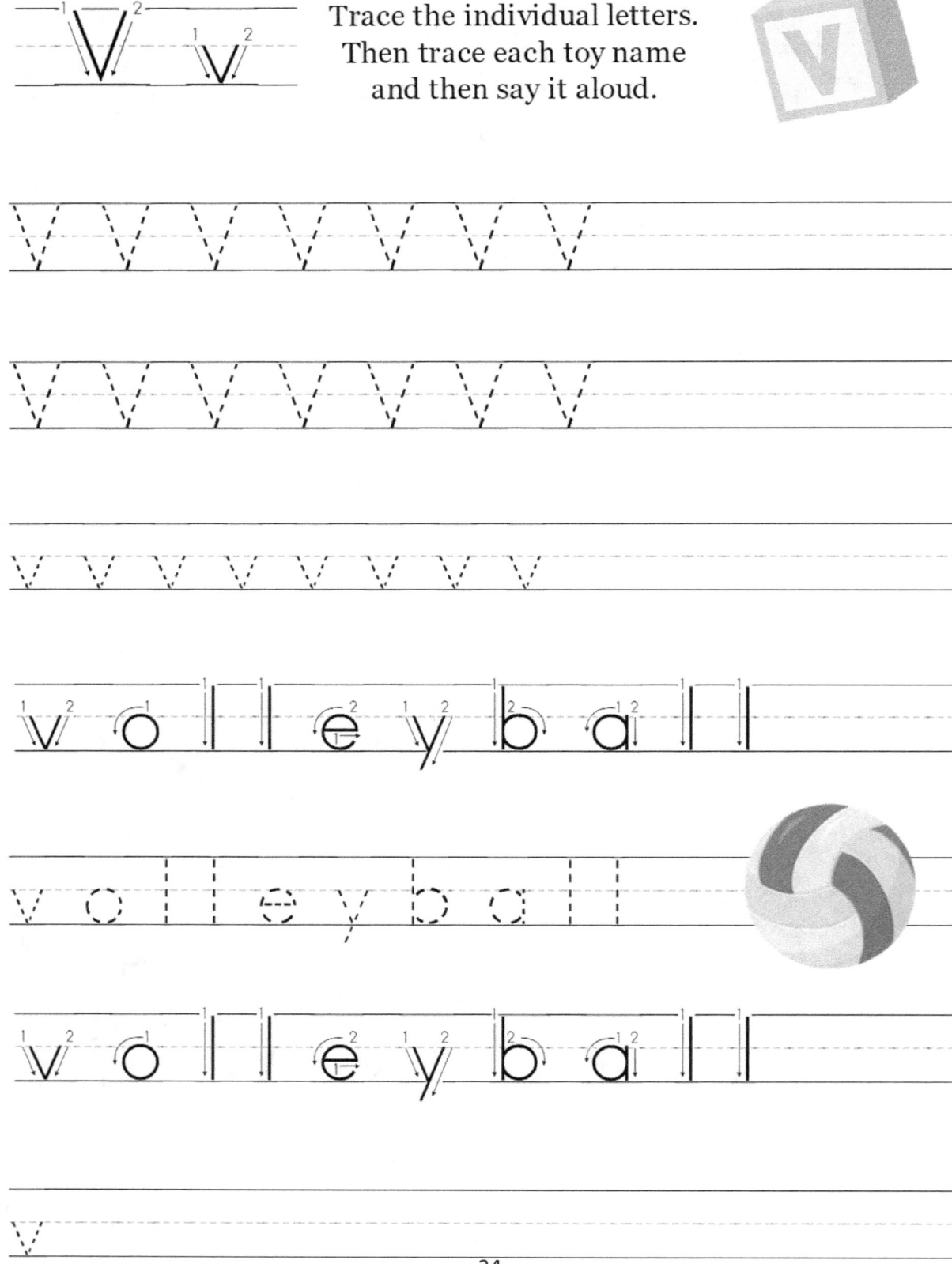

volleyball

volleyball

volleyball

Trace the individual letters.
Then trace each toy name
and then say it aloud.

W W W W

W W W W

w w w w w w w

w a n d

w a n d

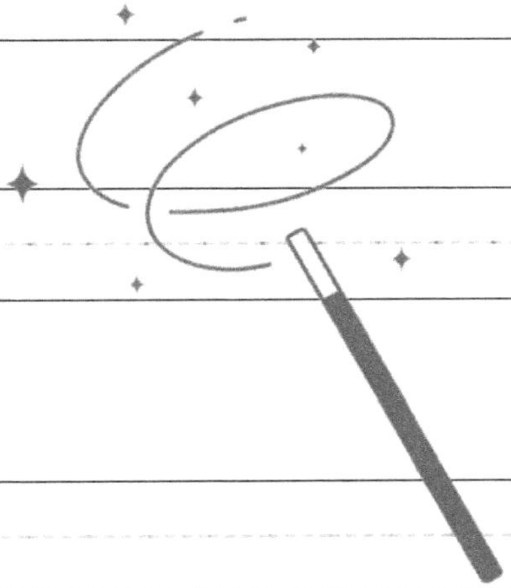

w a n d

w

WRITING WITH THE DANGER TWINS

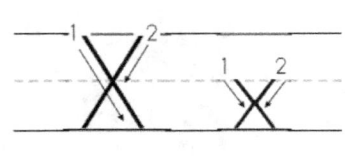

Trace the individual letters.
Then trace each toy name
and then say it aloud.

X X X X X X X

X X X X X X X

x x x x x x x x

x y l o p h o n e

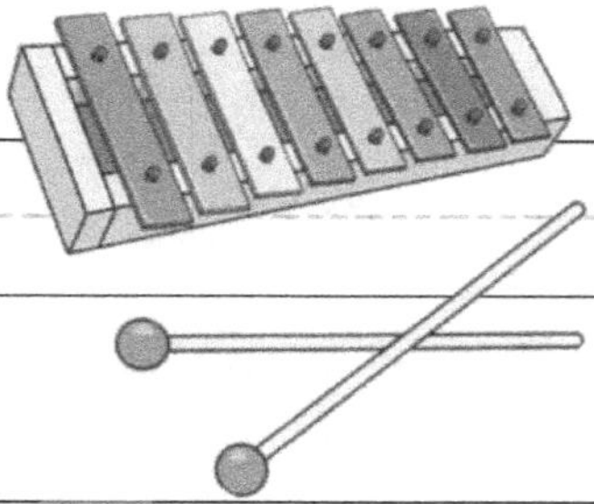

x y l o p h o n e

x y l o p h o n e

x

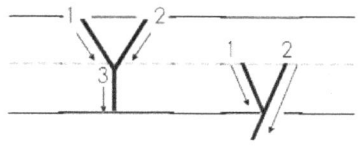

Trace the individual letters.
Then trace each toy name
and then say it aloud.

Y Y Y Y Y Y Y

Y Y Y Y Y Y Y

Y Y Y Y Y Y Y Y

yellow duck

yellow duck

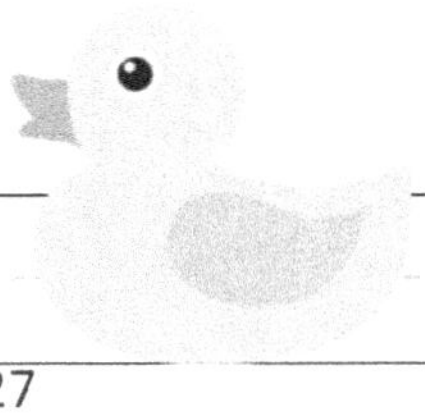

yellow duck

y

Zz Trace the individual letters.
Then trace each toy name
and then say it aloud.

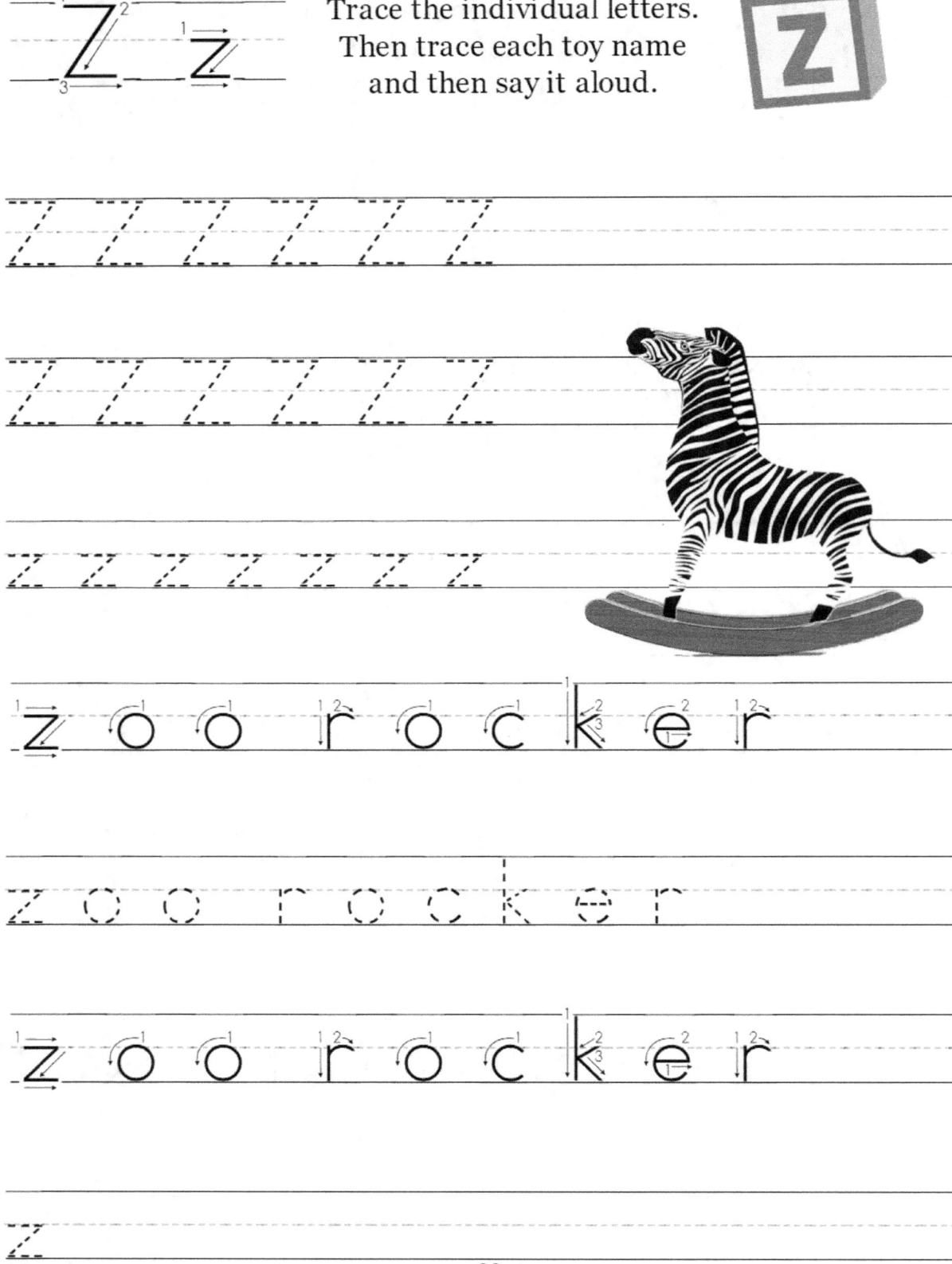

Z Z Z Z Z Z

Z Z Z Z Z Z

Z Z Z Z Z Z Z

zoo rocker

zoo rocker

zoo rocker

z

The Danger Twins listed their favorite toys. Write your favorite toys from the first section of this book.

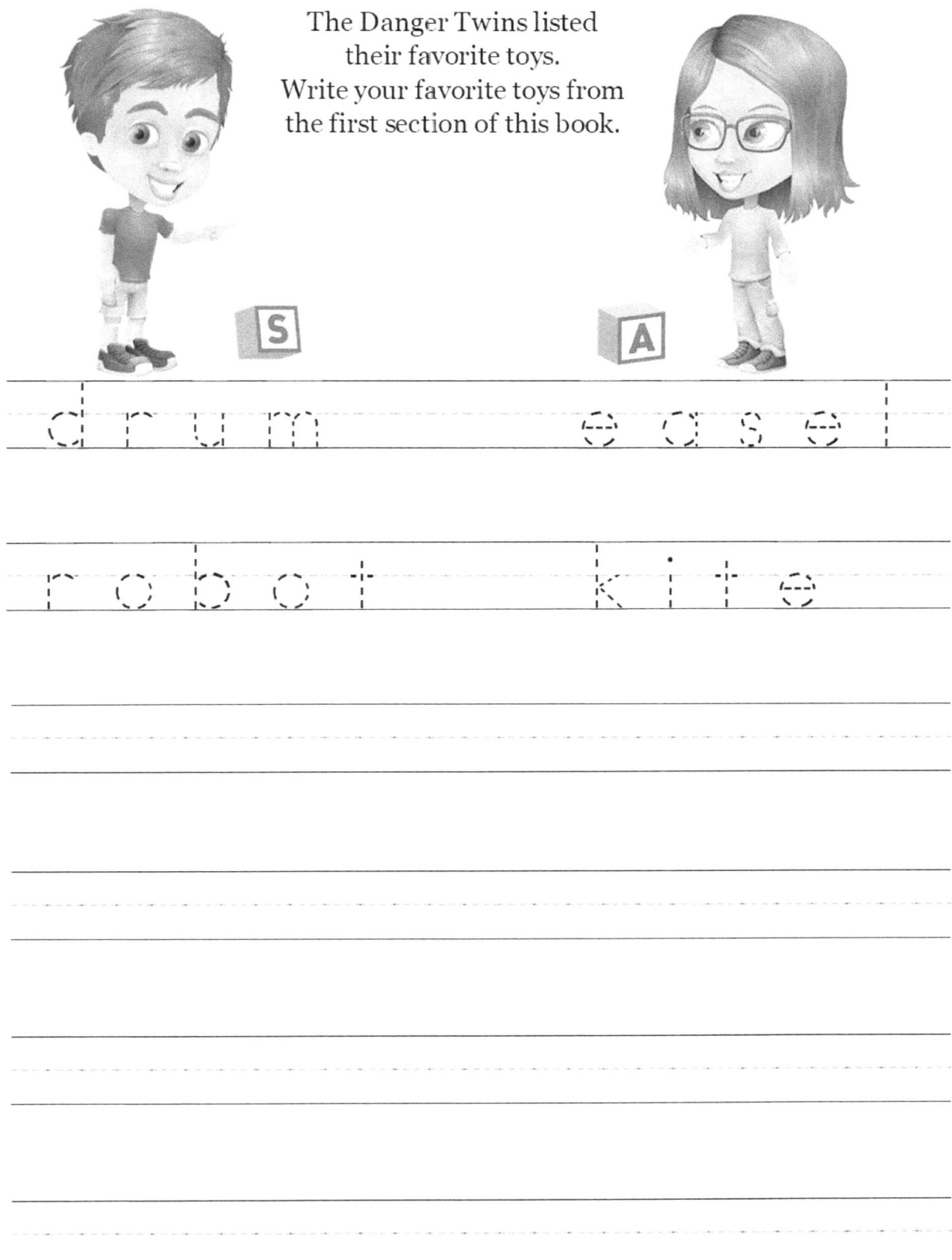

S drum   easel

A robot   kite

WRITING WITH THE DANGER TWINS

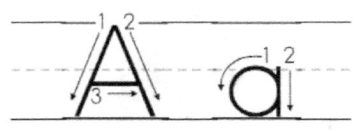

Trace the individual letters. Then trace each toy name and then say it aloud.

a a a a a a a a

a a a a a a a a

A A A A A A A A

airplane

airplane

airplane

a

WRITING WITH THE DANGER TWINS

B b

Trace the individual letters.
Then trace each toy name
and then say it aloud.

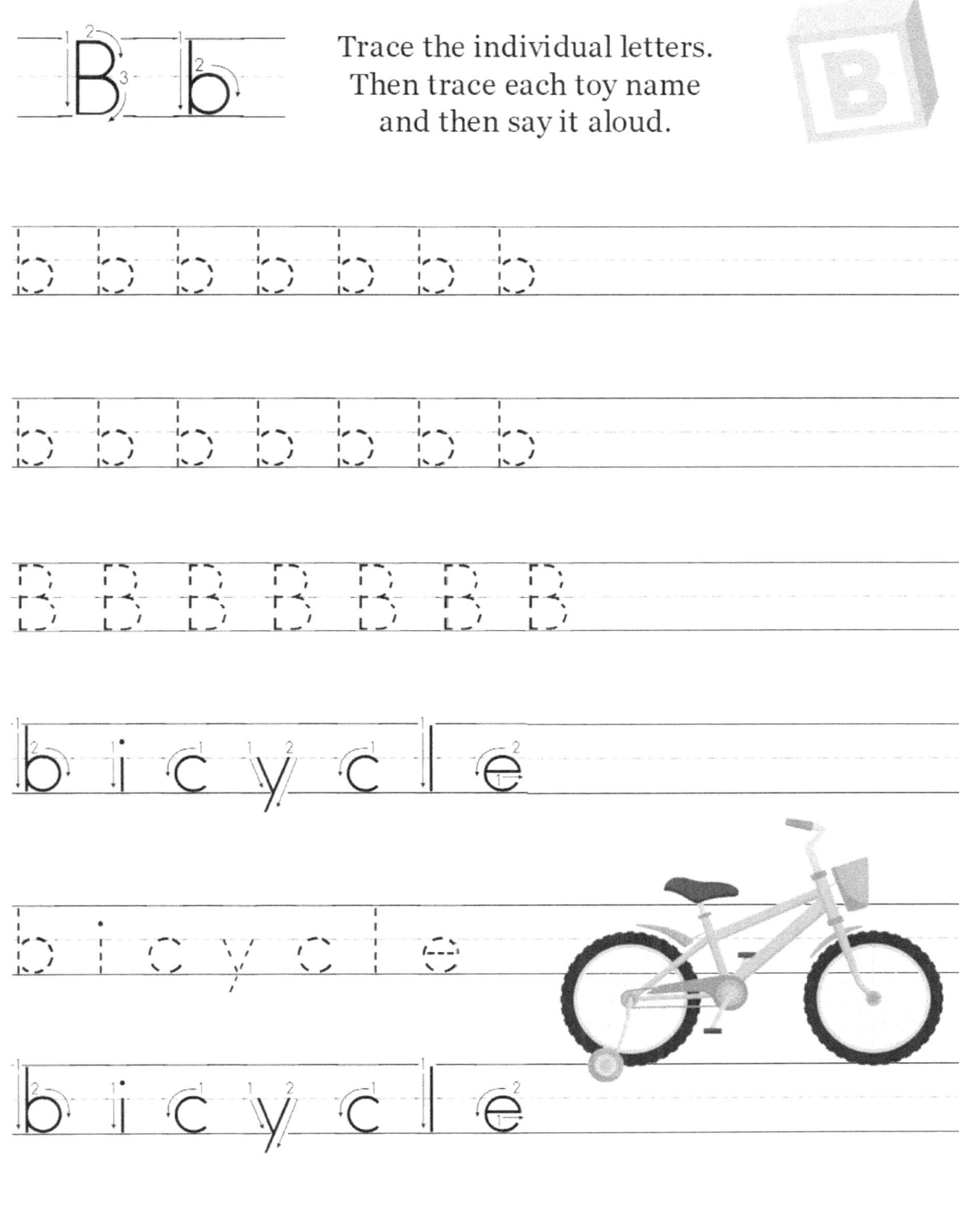

b b b b b b b

b b b b b b

B B B B B B

bicycle

bicycle

bicycle

b

C c   Trace the individual letters.
Then trace each toy name
and then say it aloud.

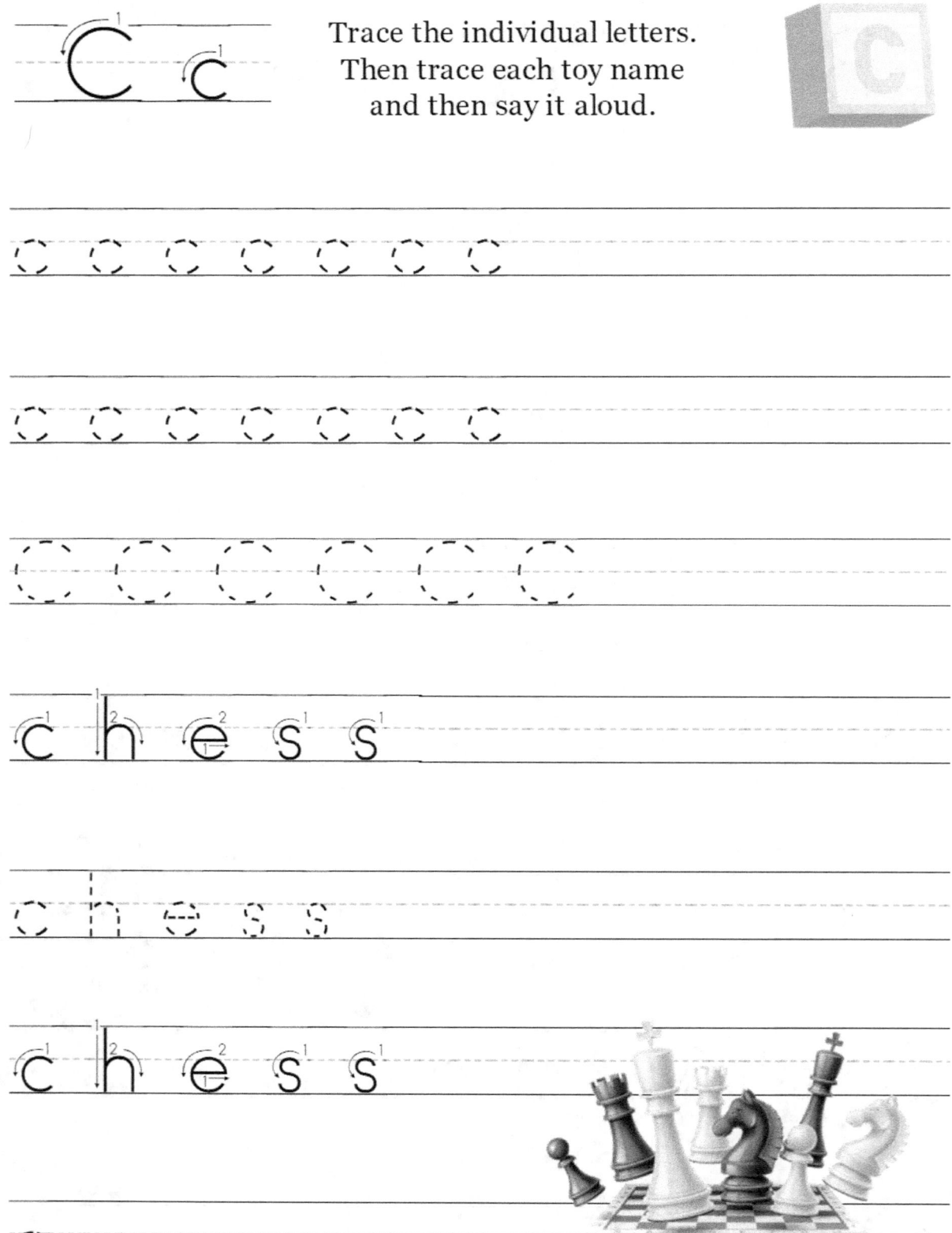

c c c c c c c

c c c c c c c

c c c c c c c

c h e s s

c h e s s

c h e s s

c

32

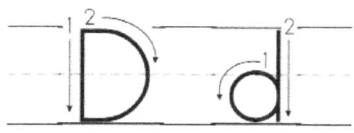

Trace the individual letters.
Then trace each toy name
and then say it aloud.

d d d d d d d

d d d d d d d

D D D D D D D

d a r t s

d a r t s

d a r t s

d

WRITING WITH THE DANGER TWINS

E e

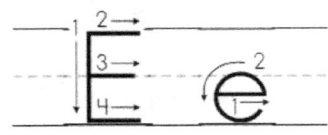

Trace the individual letters.
Then trace each toy name
and then say it aloud.

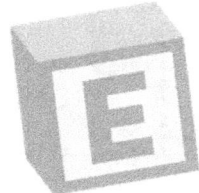

e e e e e e e

e e e e e e e

E E E E E E E

excavator

excavator

excavator

e

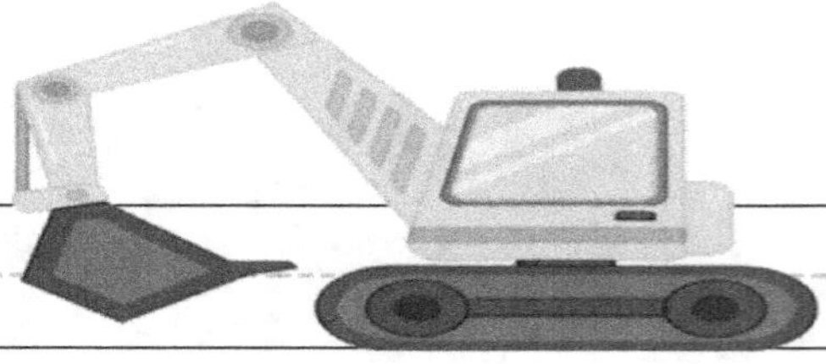

WRITING WITH THE DANGER TWINS

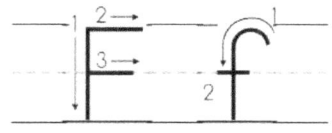

Trace the individual letters.
Then trace each toy name
and then say it aloud.

f f f f f f f

f f f f f f f

F F F F F F

f o o t b a l l

f o o t b a l l

f o o t b a l l

f

WRITING WITH THE DANGER TWINS

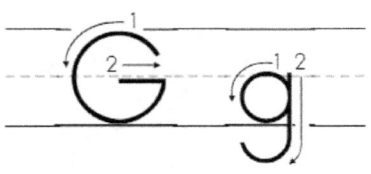 Trace the individual letters. Then trace each toy name and then say it aloud.

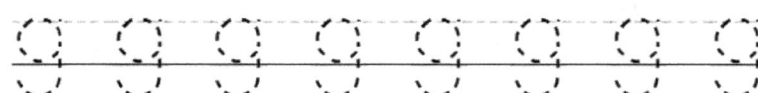

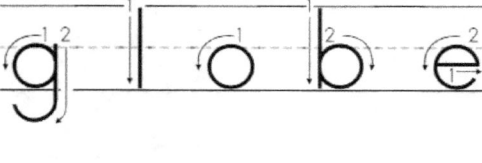

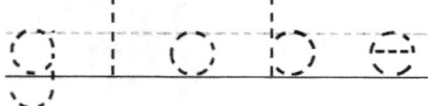

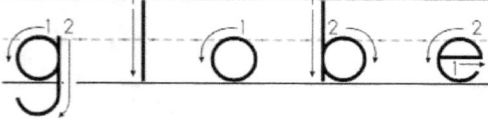

Trace the individual letters.
Then trace each toy name
and then say it aloud.

h h h h h h h

h h h h h h h

H H H H H H H

hopscotch

hopscotch

hopscotch

h

WRITING WITH THE DANGER TWINS

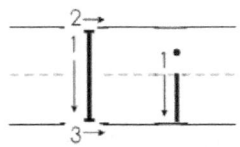

Trace the individual letters.
Then trace each toy name
and then say it aloud.

ice-skates

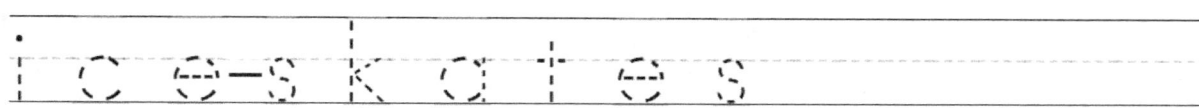

ice-skates

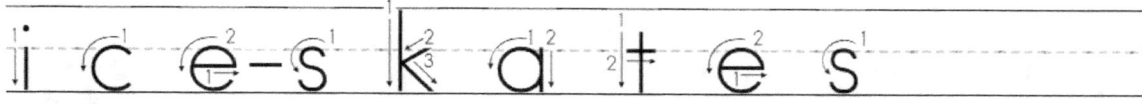

ice-skates

J j

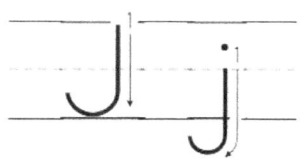

Trace the individual letters.
Then trace each toy name
and then say it aloud.

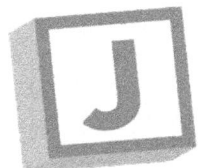

j j j j j j j j j

j j j j j j j j j

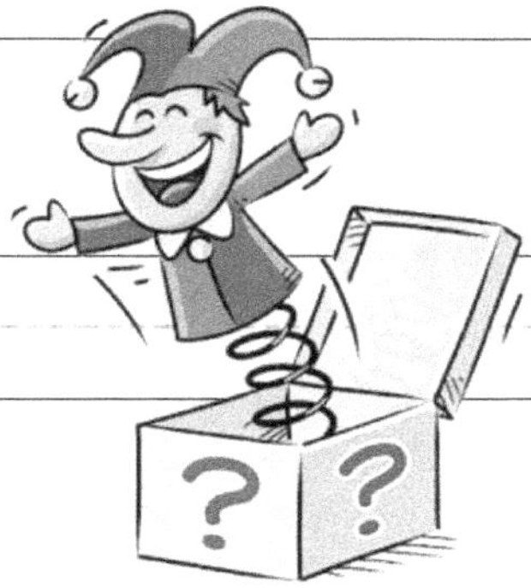

J J J J J J J

jack-in-the-box

jack-in-the-box

jack-in-the-box

j

WRITING WITH THE DANGER TWINS

K k

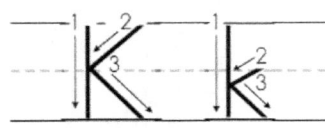

Trace the individual letters.
Then trace each toy name
and then say it aloud.

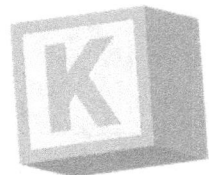

k k k k k k k k

k k k k k k k k

K K K K K K K

kaleidoscope

kaleidoscope

kaleidoscope

k

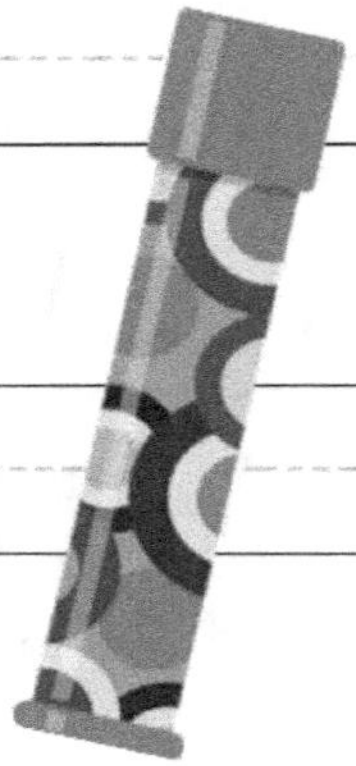

WRITING WITH THE DANGER TWINS

Trace the individual letters.
Then trace each toy name
and then say it aloud.

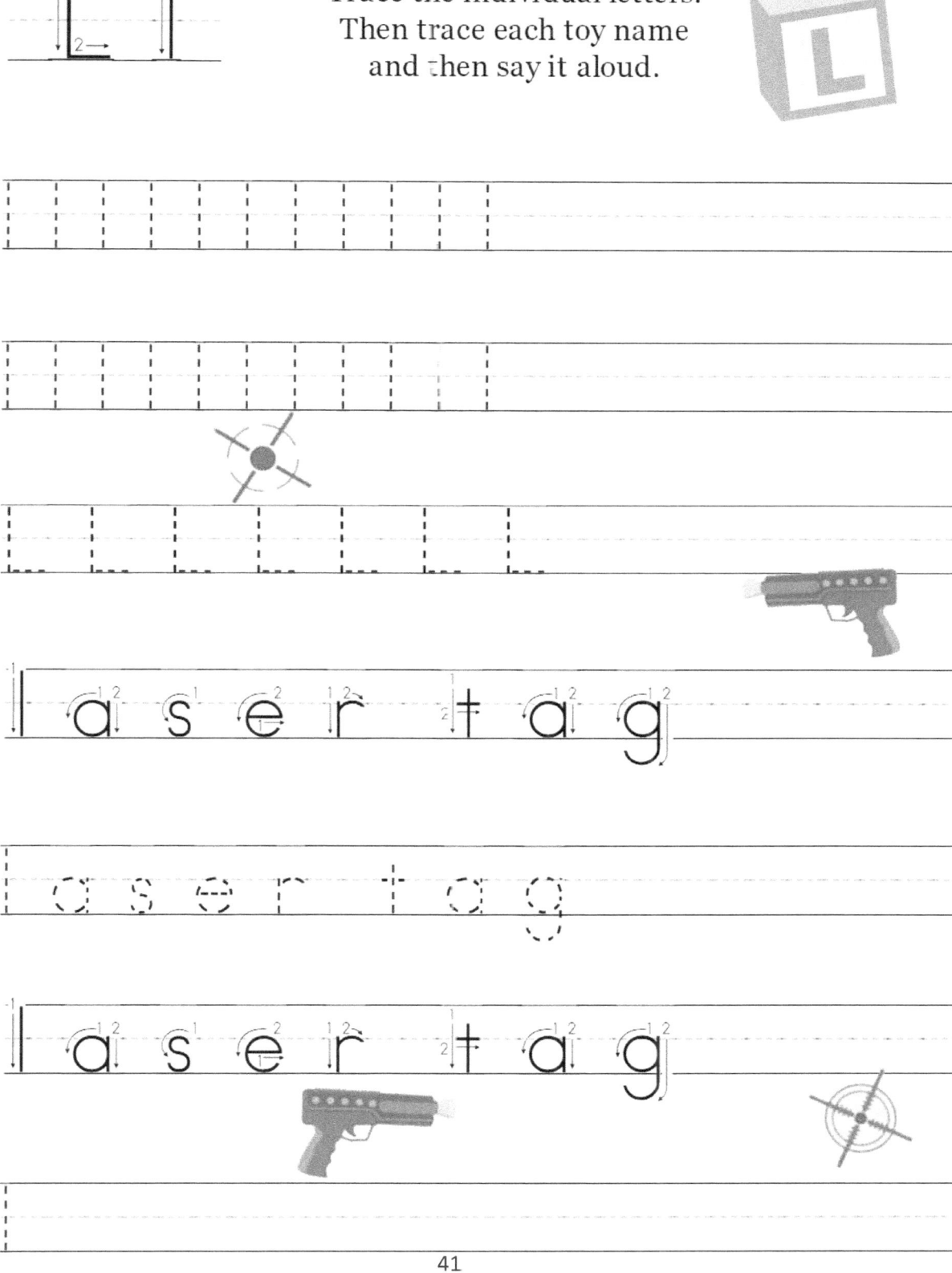

l a s e r   t a g

l a s e r   t a g

l a s e r   t a g

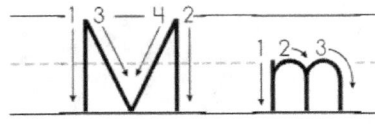 

Trace the individual letters.
Then trace each toy name
and then say it aloud.

m m m m m m m m

m m m m m m m m

M M M M M M M

marbles

marbles

marbles

m

WRITING WITH THE DANGER TWINS

N n

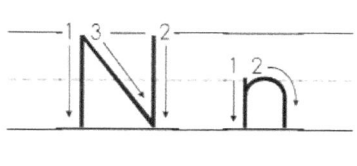

Trace the individual letters.
Then trace each toy name
and then say it aloud.

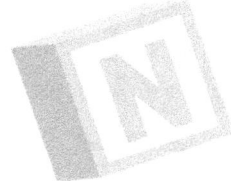

n n n n n n n n

n n n n n n n n

N N N N N N

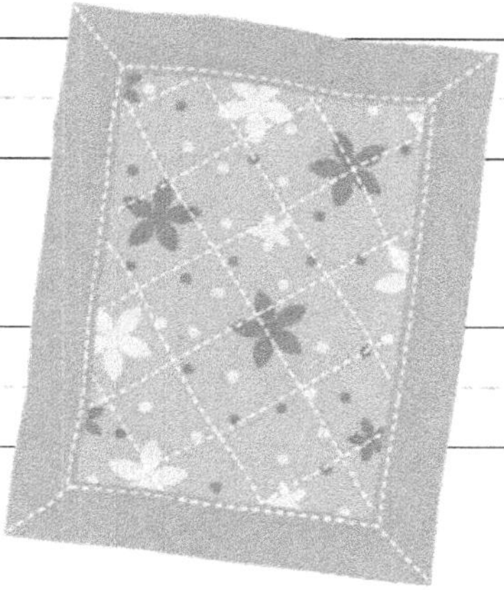

nap blanket

nap blanket

nap blanket

n

Trace the individual letters.
Then trace each toy name
and then say it aloud.

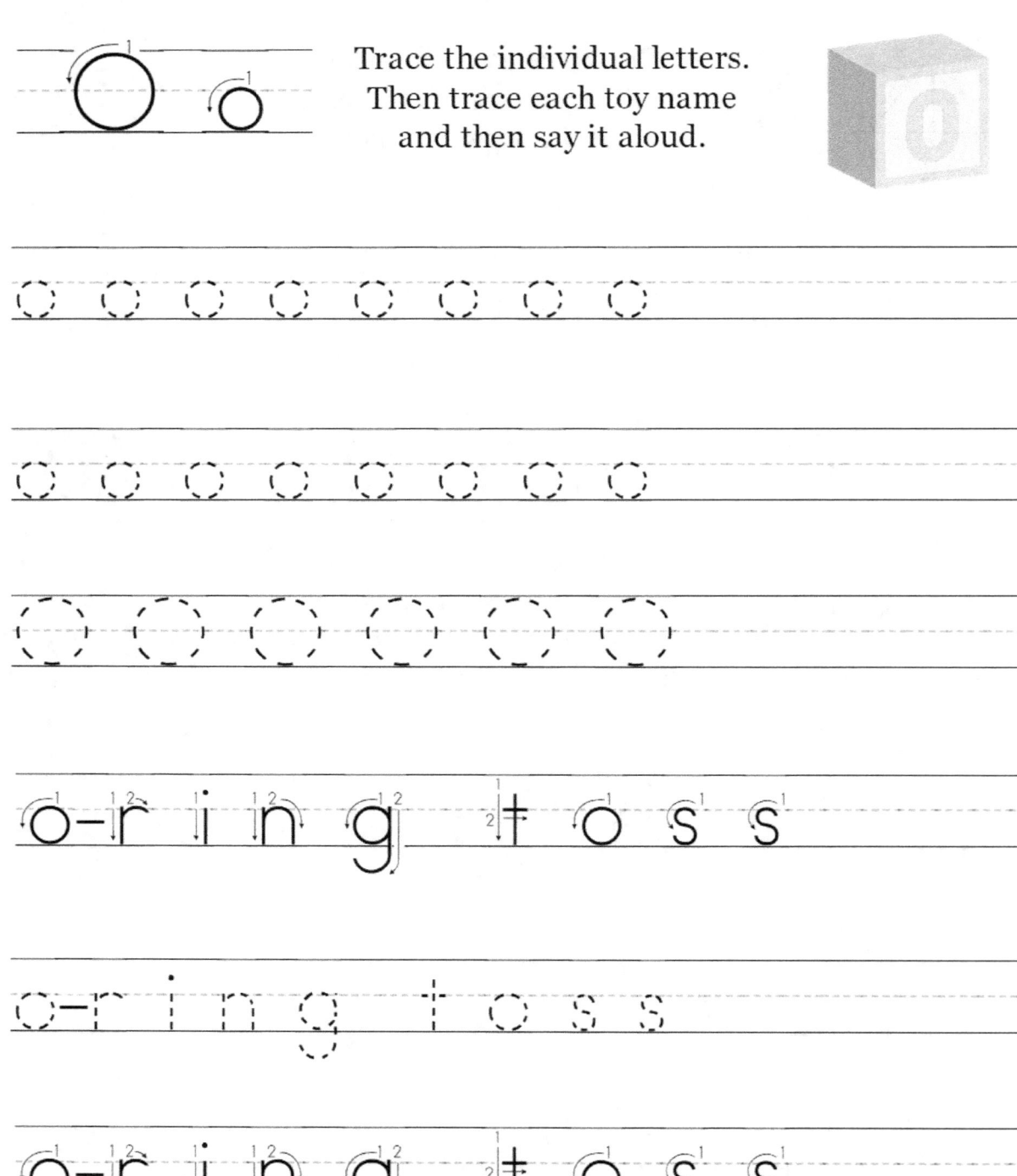

o-ring toss

o-ring toss

o-ring toss

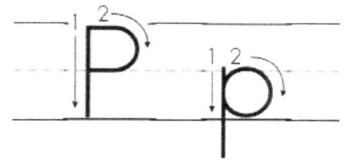

Trace the individual letters.
Then trace each toy name
and then say it aloud.

P P P P P P

P P P P P P

P P P P P P

p o g o s t i c k

p o g o s t i c k

p o g o s t i c k

p

45

WRITING WITH THE DANGER TWINS

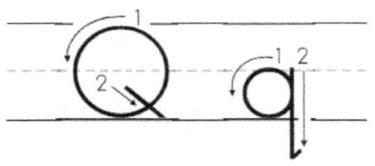

Trace the individual letters.
Then trace each toy name
and then say it aloud.

q q q q q q q

q q q q q q q

Q Q Q Q Q Q

quiz game

quiz game

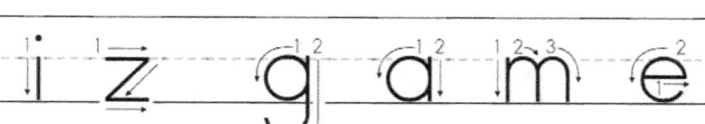

quiz game

q

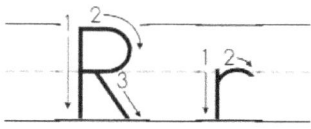

Trace the individual letters.
Then trace each toy name
and then say it aloud.

r r r r r r r

r r r r r r r

R R R R R R

rattle

rattle

rattle

r

WRITING WITH THE DANGER TWINS

Trace the individual letters.
Then trace each toy name
and then say it aloud.

S S S S S S S S

S S S S S S S

S S S S S S

s w i n g

s w i n g

s w i n g

s

WRITING WITH THE DANGER TWINS

Trace the individual letters. Then trace each toy name and then say it aloud.

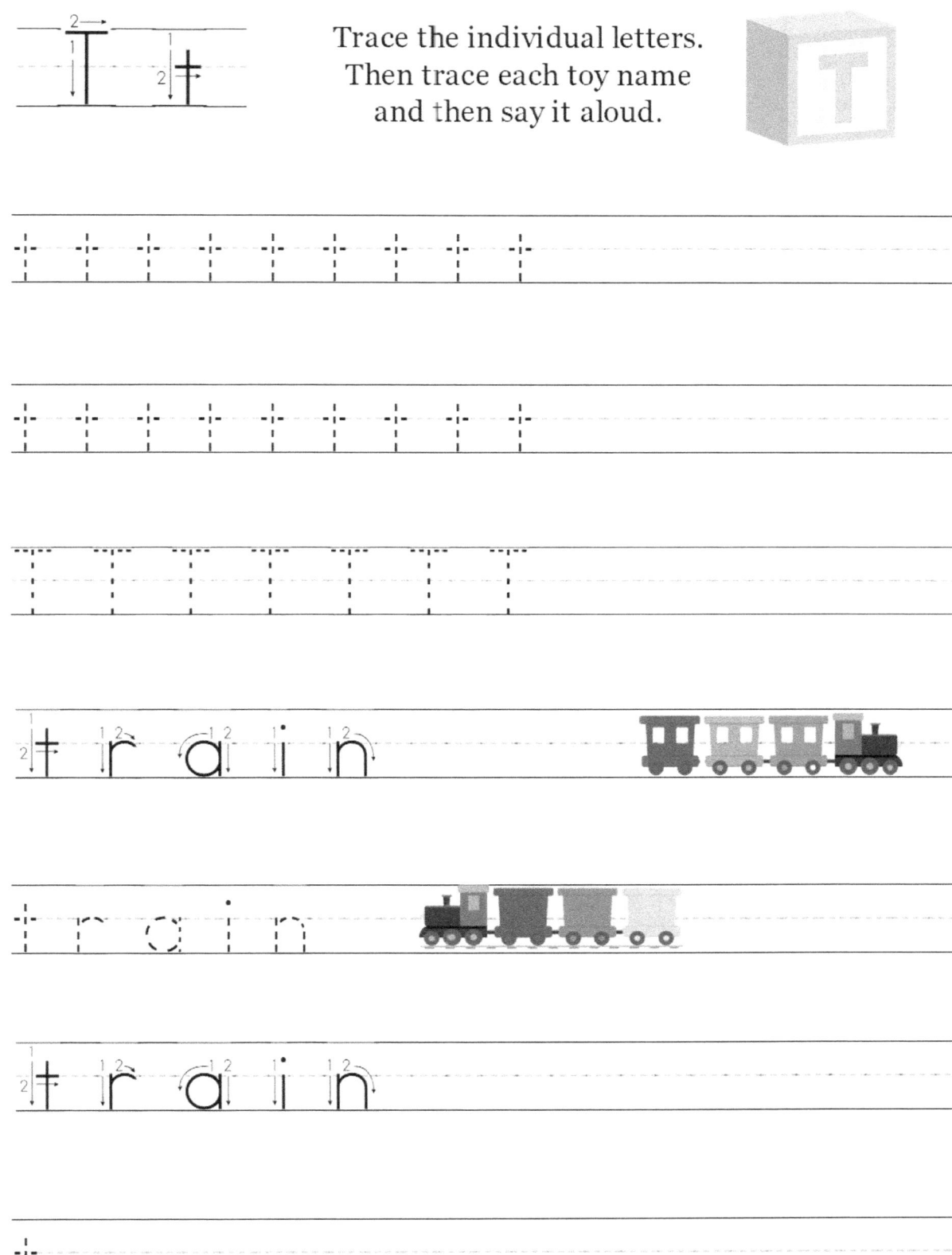

Trace the individual letters.
Then trace each toy name
and then say it aloud.

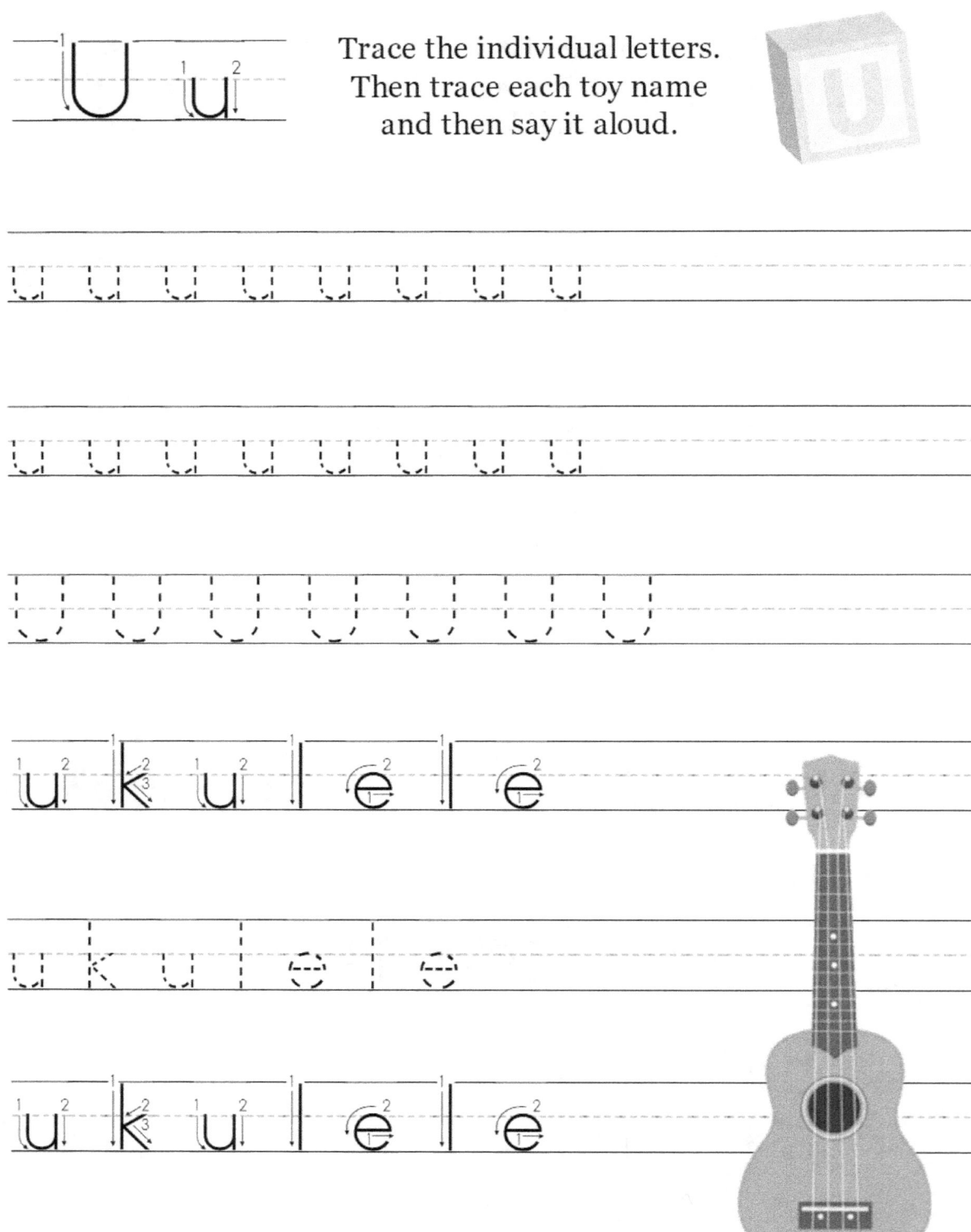

U U U U U U U U

U U U U U U U U

U U U U U U U

ukulele ele

ukulele ele

ukulele ele

U

Trace the individual letters.
Then trace each toy name
and then say it aloud.

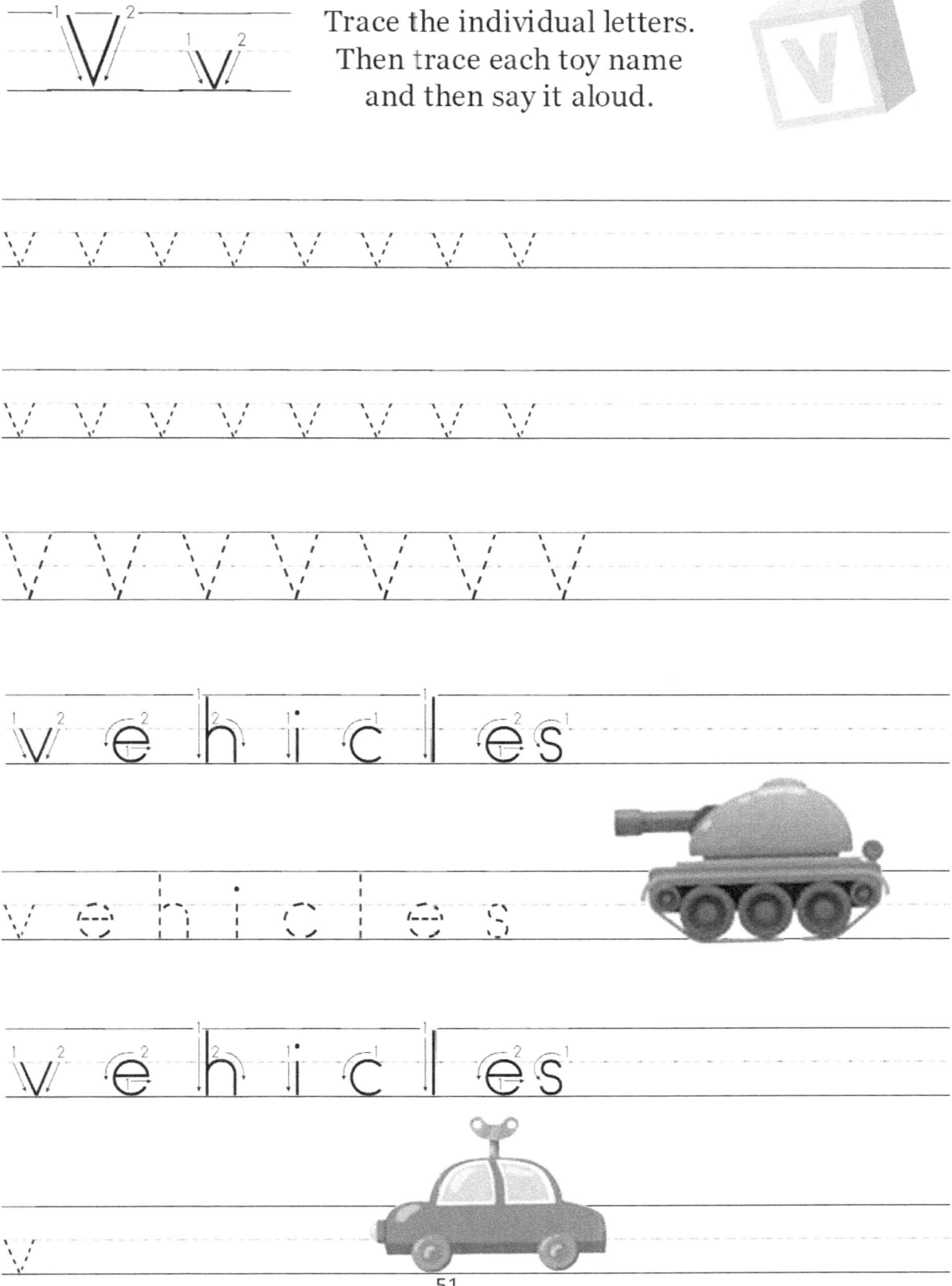

V V V V V V V

V V V V V V V

V V V V V V V

vehicles

vehicles

vehicles

v

WRITING WITH THE DANGER TWINS

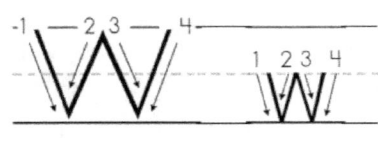 Trace the individual letters.
Then trace each toy name
and then say it aloud.

w w w w w w w w

w w w w w w w w

w w w w w

wagon

wagon

wagon

w

WRITING WITH THE DANGER TWINS

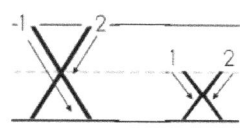

Trace the individual letters.
Then trace each toy name
and then say it aloud.

X X X X X X X X

X X X X X X X X

X X X X X X

x-map

x-map

x-map

X

WRITING WITH THE DANGER TWINS

Trace the individual letters. Then trace each toy name and then say it aloud.

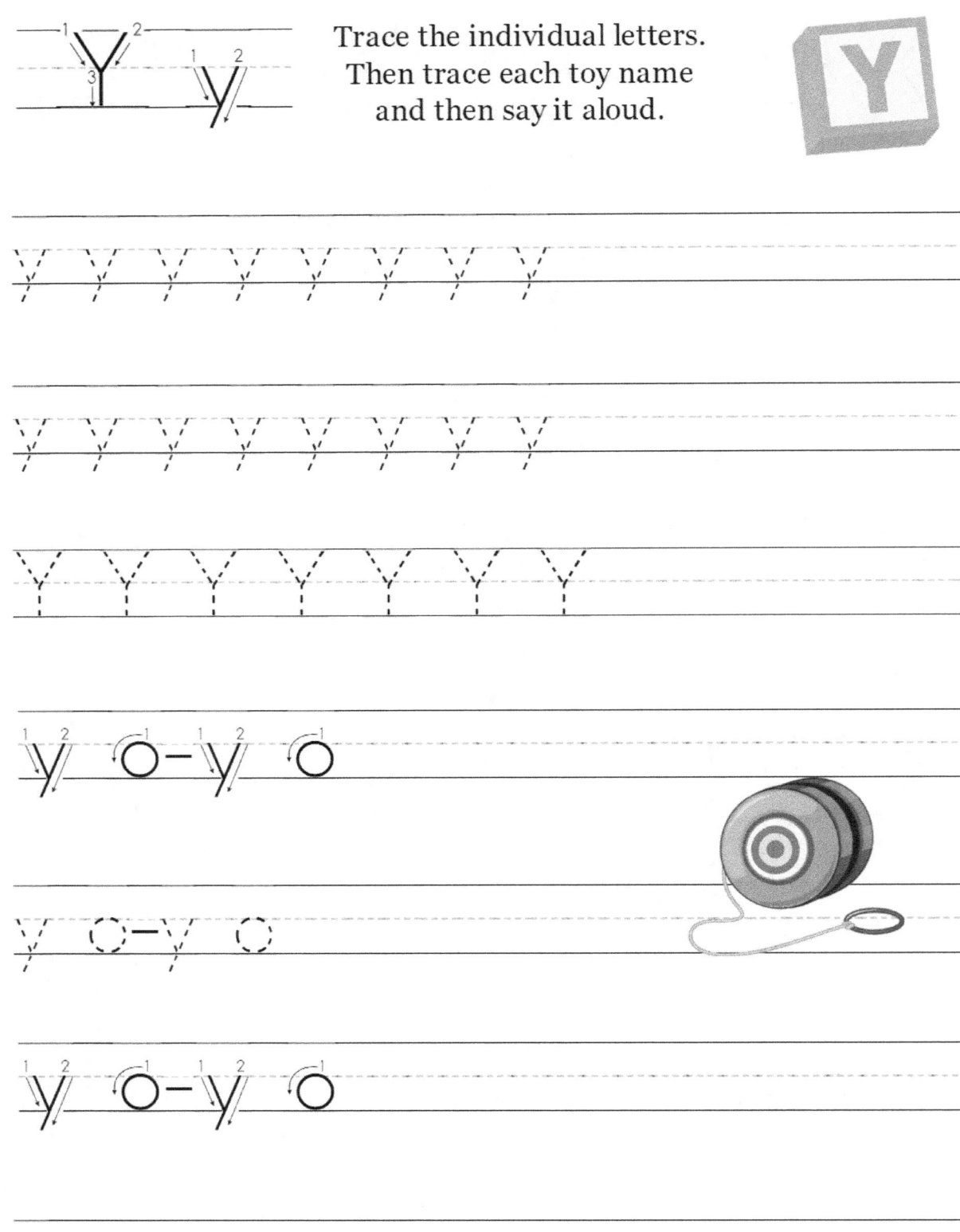

WRITING WITH THE DANGER TWINS

Zz   Trace the individual letters. Then trace each toy name and then say it aloud.

Z

z z z z z z z

z z z z z z z

z z z z z z z

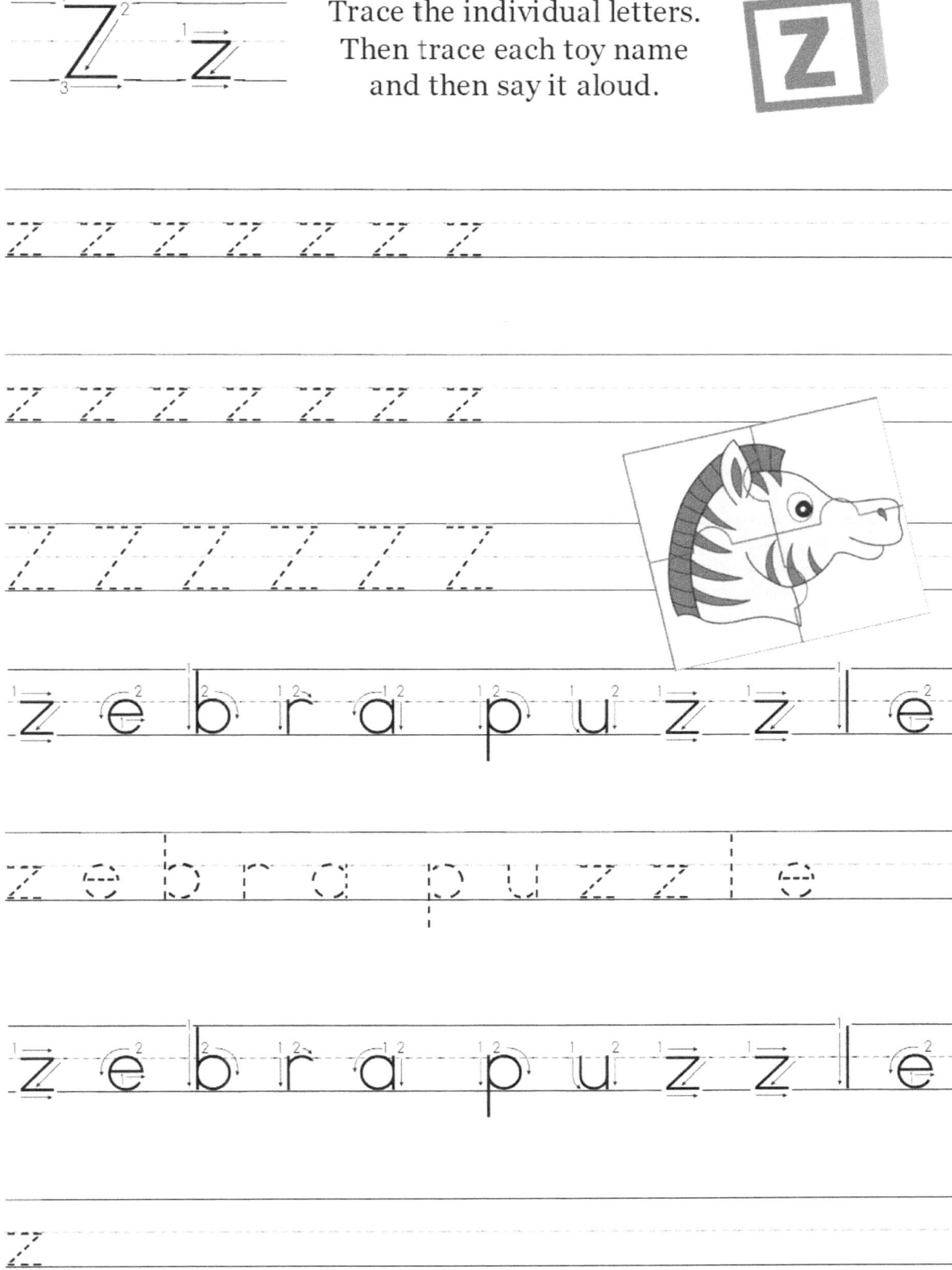

zebra puzzle

zebra puzzle

zebra puzzle

z

The Danger Twins listed
their favorite toys.
Write your favorite toys from
the second section of this book.

bicycle   chess

globe   train

WRITING WITH THE DANGER TWINS

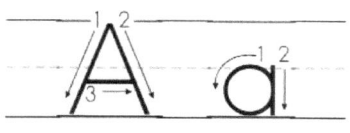

Trace the individual letters. Then trace each toy name and then say it aloud.

A A A A A A A A

A

a a a a a a a a

a

A B C b l o c k s

A B C b l o c k s

A B C b l o c k s

WRITING WITH THE DANGER TWINS

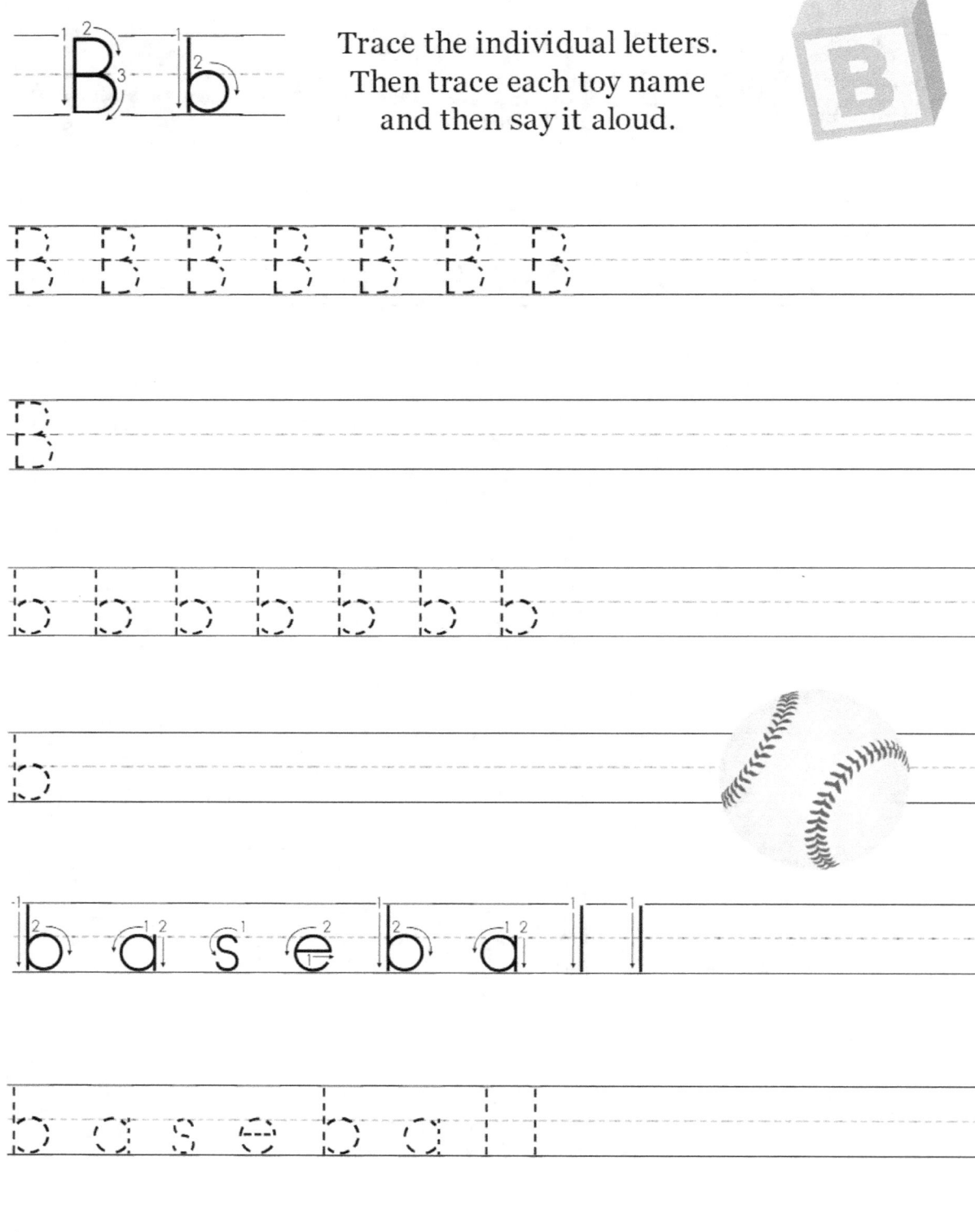

Trace the individual letters.
Then trace each toy name
and then say it aloud.

B B B B B B B

B

b b b b b b b

b

baseball

baseball

baseball

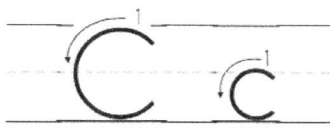

Trace the individual letters.
Then trace each toy name
and then say it aloud.

C C C C C C

C

c c c c c c

c

c h e c k e r s

c h e c k e r s

c h e c k e r s

Trace the individual letters.
Then trace each toy name
and then say it aloud.

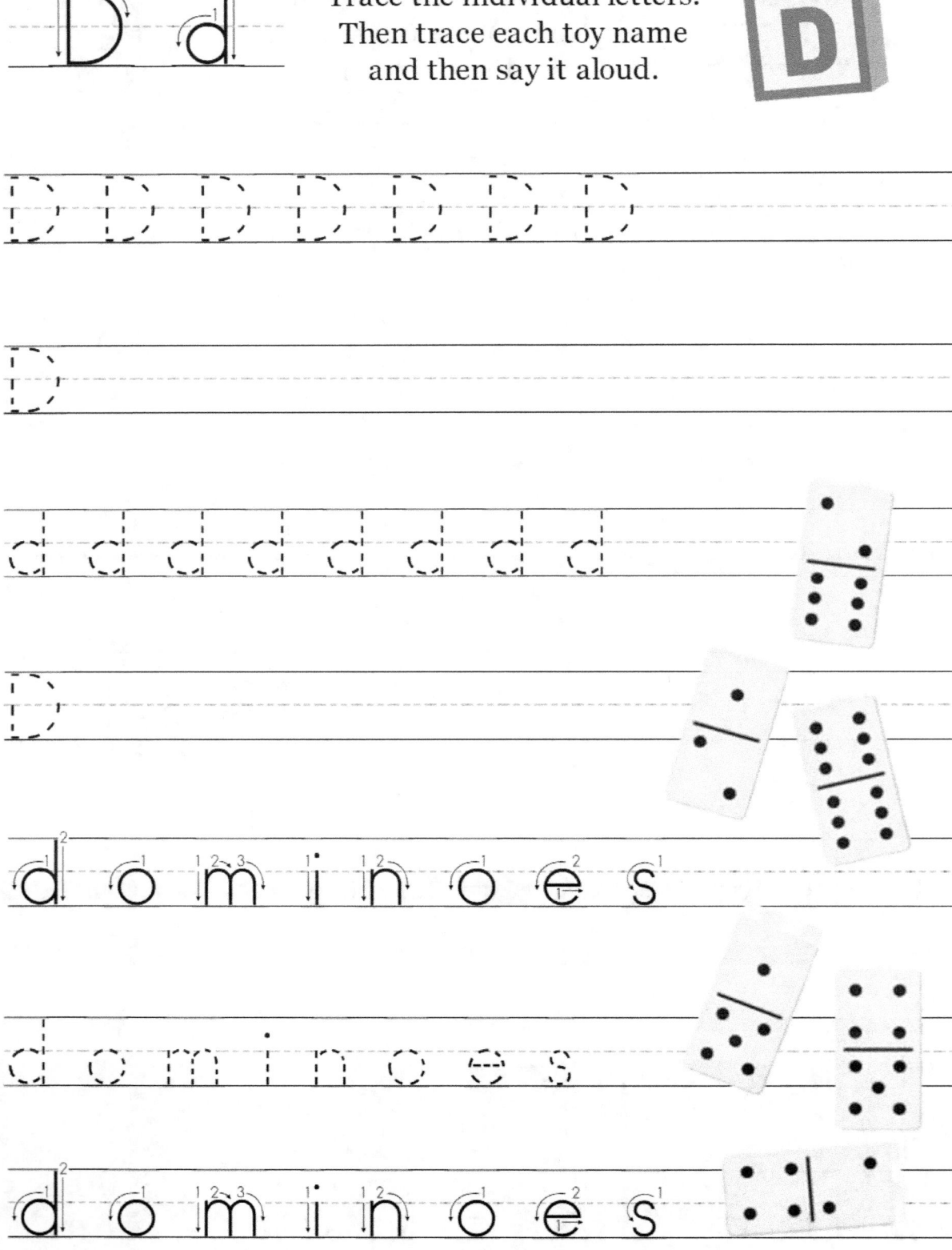

D D D D D D D

D

d d d d d d d

D

dominoes

dominoes

dominoes

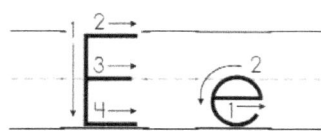

Trace the individual letters.
Then trace each toy name
and then say it aloud.

E E E E E E E

E

e e e e e e e

e

engine

engine

engine

61

WRITING WITH THE DANGER TWINS

F f

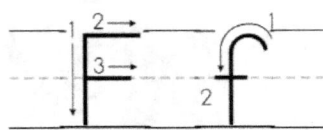

Trace the individual letters.
Then trace each toy name
and then say it aloud.

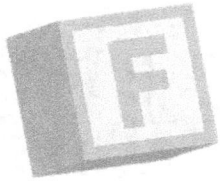

F F F F F F F

F

f f f f f f f f

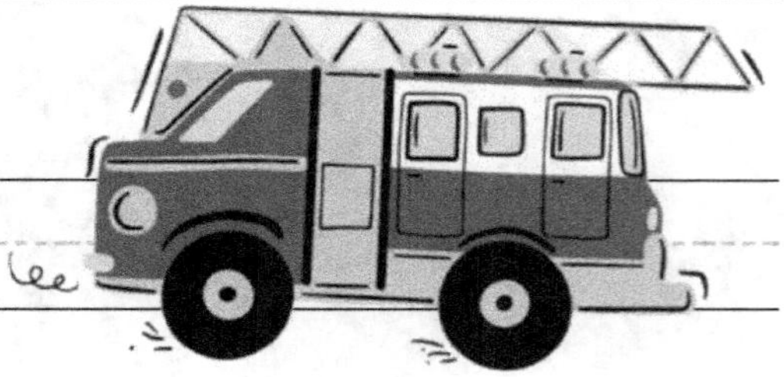

f

fire truck

fire truck

fire truck

WRITING WITH THE DANGER TWINS

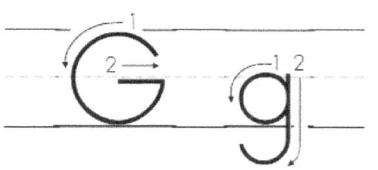

Trace the individual letters. Then trace each toy name and then say it aloud.

G G G G G G

G

g g g g g g g g

g

g o g g l e s

g o g g l e s

g o g g l e s

WRITING WITH THE DANGER TWINS

Trace the individual letters.
Then trace each toy name
and then say it aloud.

h e l i c o p t e r

h e l i c o p t e r

h e l i c o p t e r

WRITING WITH THE DANGER TWINS

Trace the individual letters.
Then trace each toy name
and then say it aloud.

I i

inspector kit

inspector kit

inspector kit

WRITING WITH THE DANGER TWINS

J j

Trace the individual letters.
Then trace each toy name
and then say it aloud.

J

J J J J J J J J

J

j j j j j j j j

j

j a c k s

j a c k s

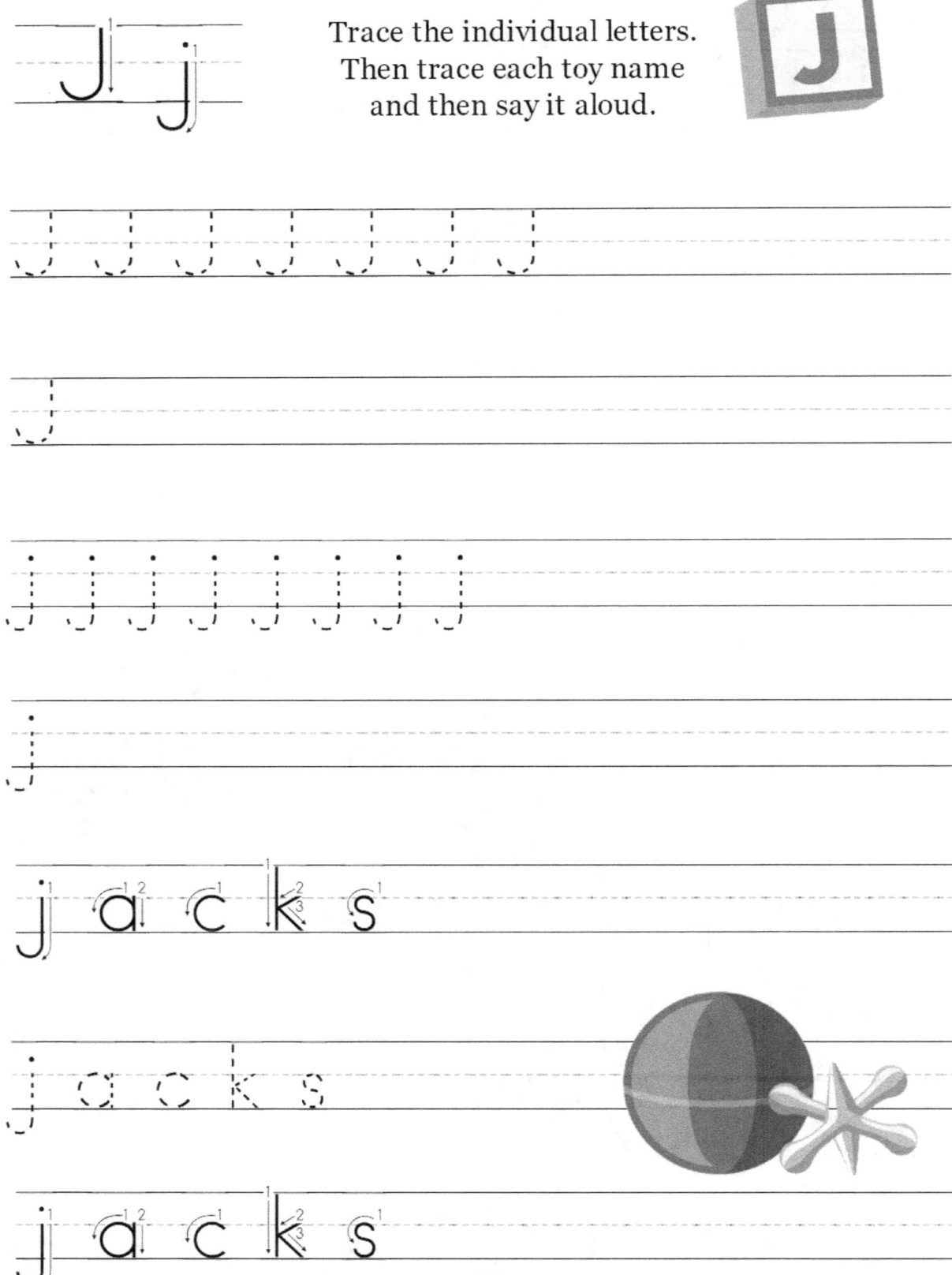

j a c k s

K k

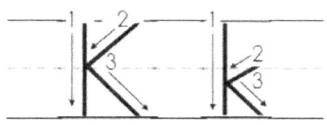

Trace the individual letters.
Then trace each toy name
and then say it aloud.

K K K K K K K

K

k k k k k k k k

k

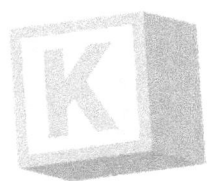

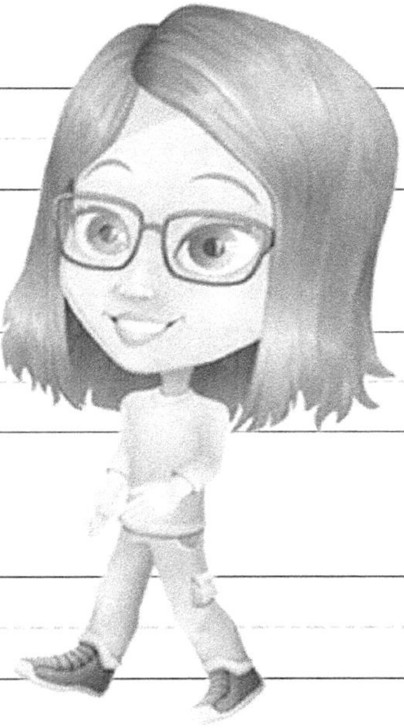

kickball

kickball

kickball

WRITING WITH THE DANGER TWINS

Trace the individual letters.
Then trace each toy name
and then say it aloud.

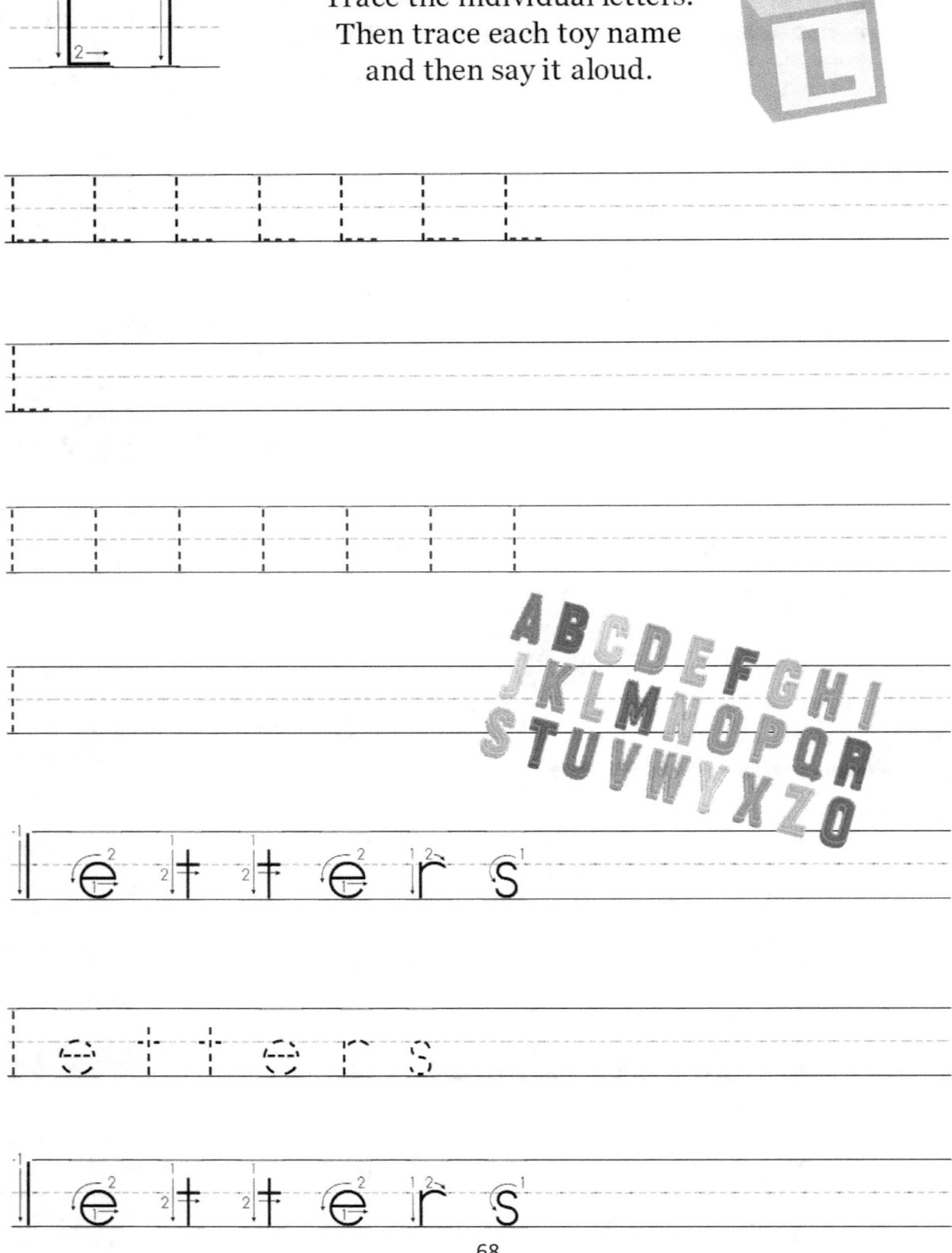

letters

letters

letters

WRITING WITH THE DANGER TWINS

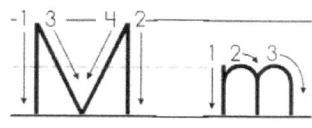

Trace the individual letters.
Then trace each toy name
and then say it aloud.

M M M M M

M

m m m m m m

m

monster truck

monster truck

monster truck

WRITING WITH THE DANGER TWINS

N n

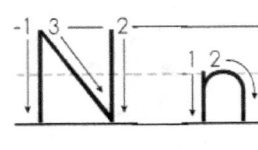

Trace the individual letters.
Then trace each toy name
and then say it aloud.

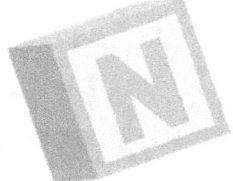

N N N N N N

N

n n n n n n n n

n

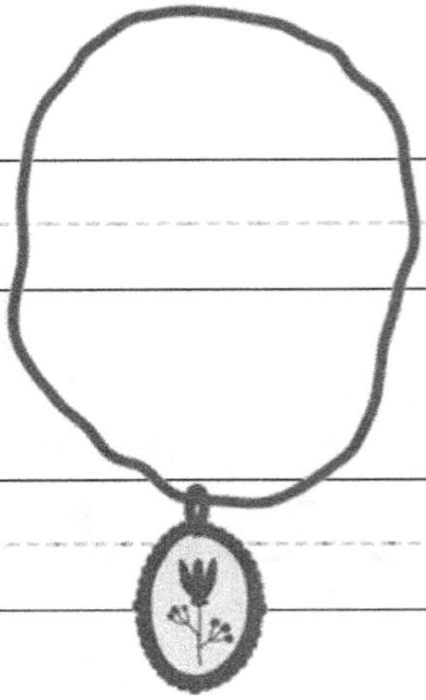

necklace

necklace

necklace

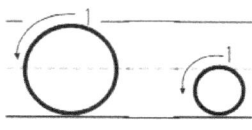

Trace the individual letters.
Then trace each toy name
and then say it aloud.

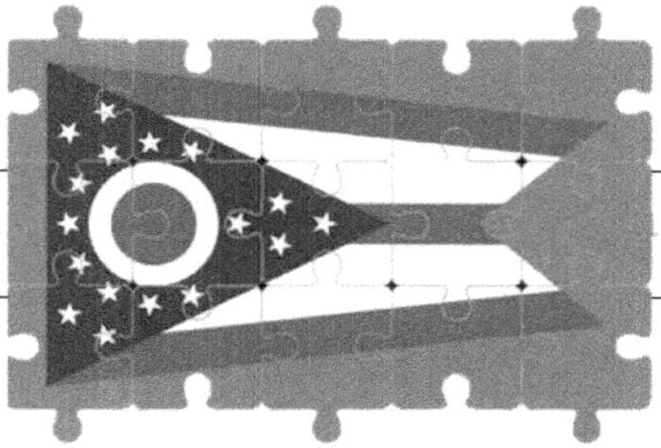

O O O O O O

O

o o o o o o o

o

Ohio puzzle

Ohio puzzle

Ohio puzzle

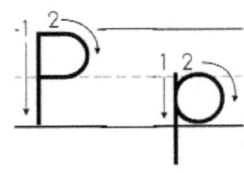

Trace the individual letters.
Then trace each toy name
and then say it aloud.

P P P P P P P

P

P P P P P P P

P

p u p p e t

p u p p e t

p u p p e t

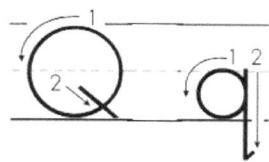

Trace the individual letters.
Then trace each toy name
and then say it aloud.

Q Q Q Q Q

Q

q q q q q q

q

questions

questions

questions

73

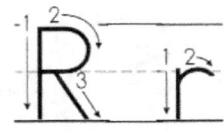

Trace the individual letters.
Then trace each toy name
and then say it aloud.

R R R R R R R

R

r r r r r r r

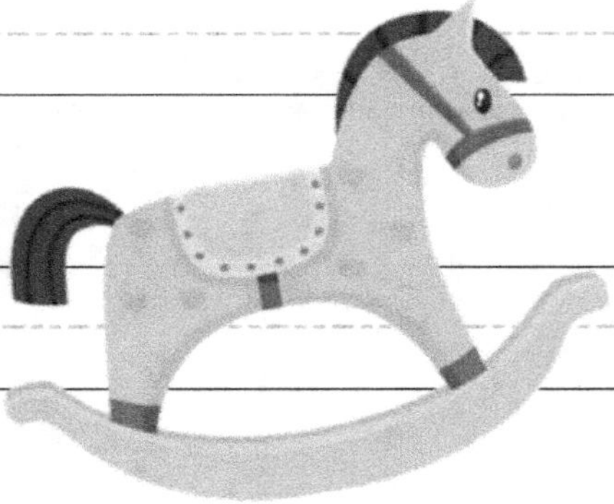

r

rocking horse

rocking horse

rocking horse

WRITING WITH THE DANGER TWINS

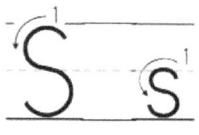

Trace the individual letters.
Then trace each toy name
and then say it aloud.

S s s s s s

s

s s s s s s s

s

slide

slide

slide

WRITING WITH THE DANGER TWINS

Trace the individual letters.
Then trace each toy name
and then say it aloud.

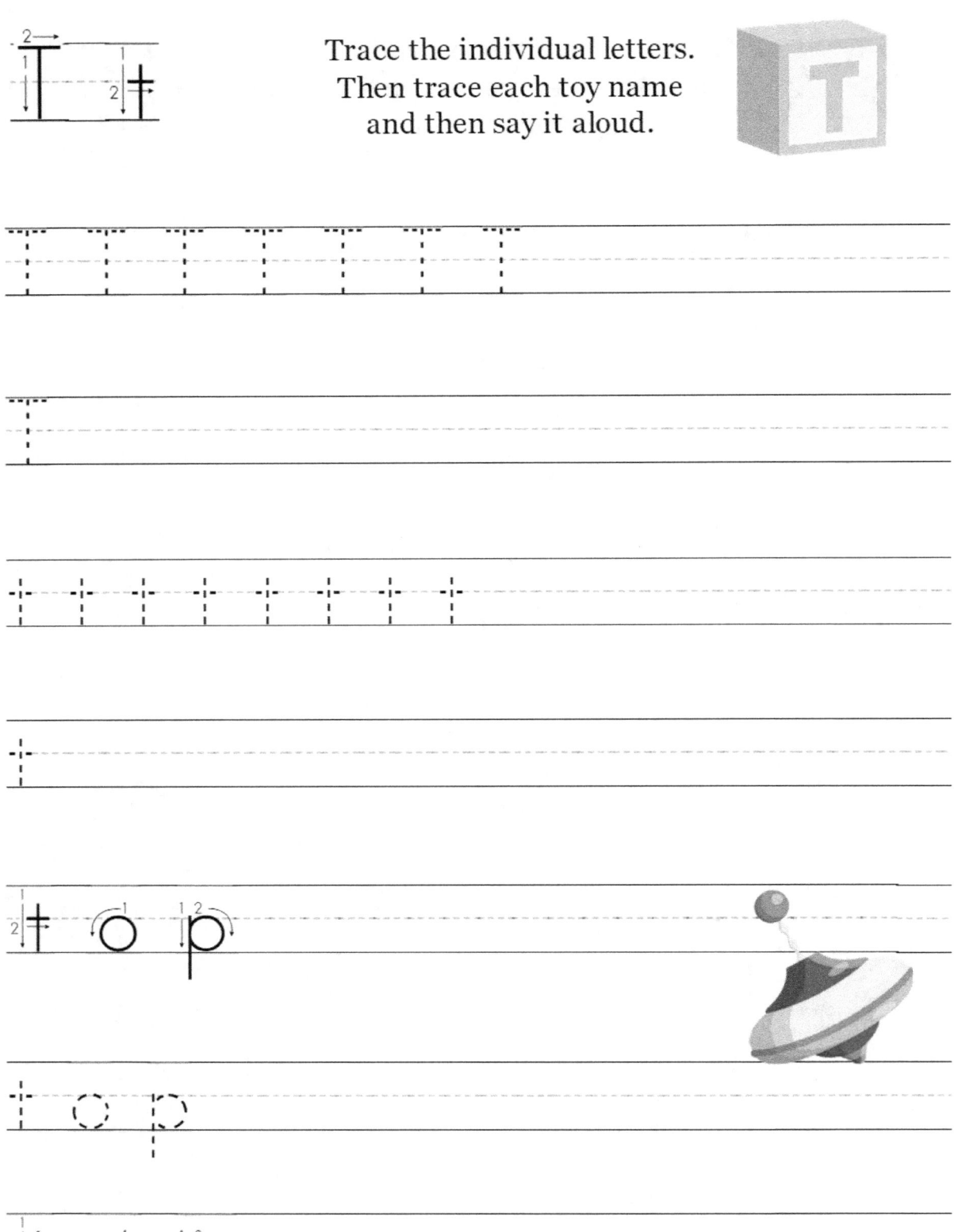

WRITING WITH THE DANGER TWINS

U u

Trace the individual letters.
Then trace each toy name
and then say it aloud.

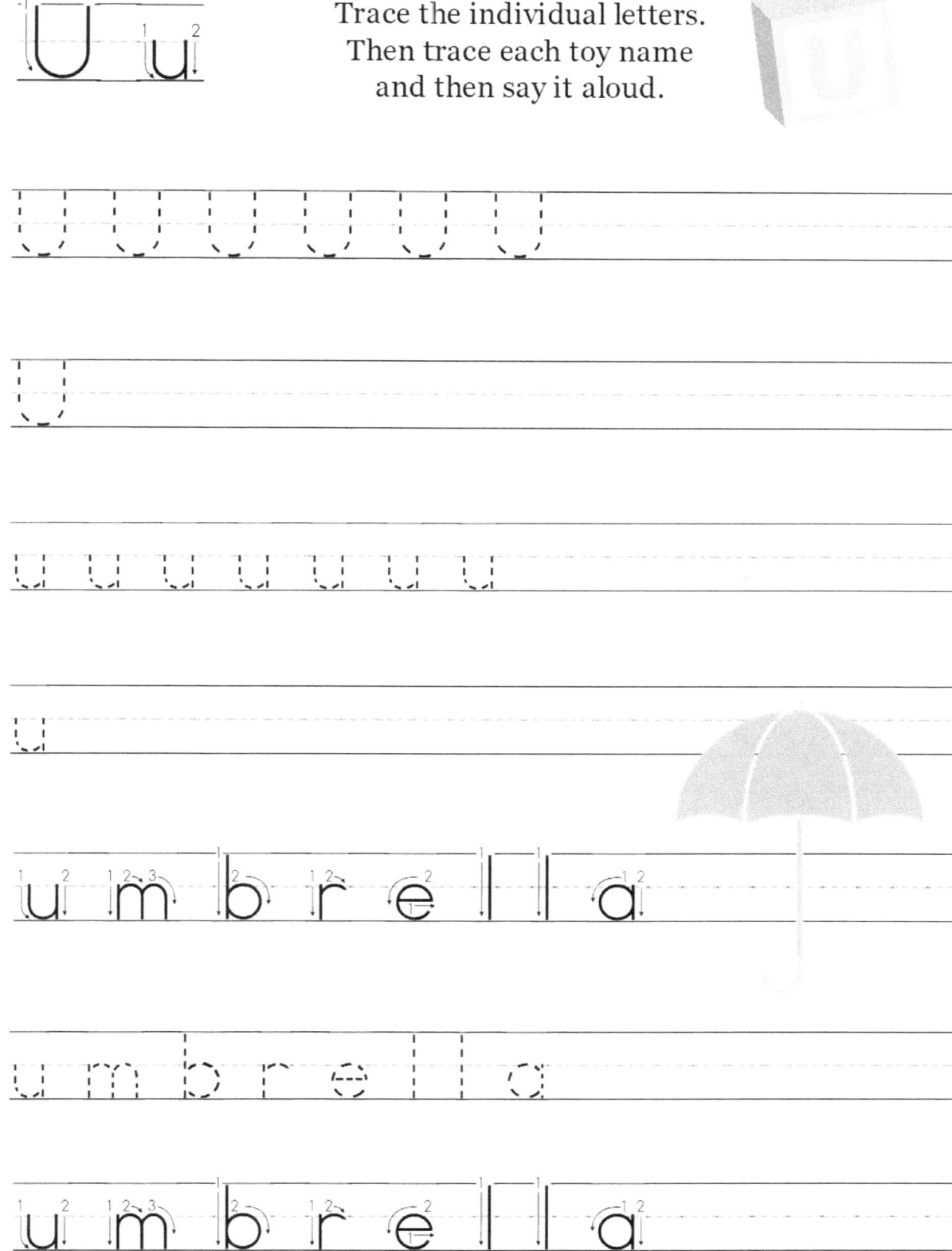

U U U U U U

U

u u u u u u u

u

umbrella

umbrella

umbrella

WRITING WITH THE DANGER TWINS

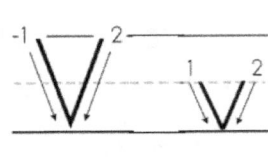

Trace the individual letters.
Then trace each toy name
and then say it aloud.

V v v v v v v v

v

v v v v v v v v

v

video game

video game

video game

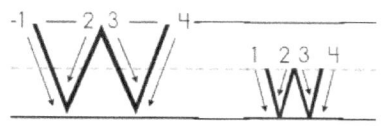

Trace the individual letters.
Then trace each toy name
and then say it aloud.

W W W W W

W

w w w w w w w

w

whistle

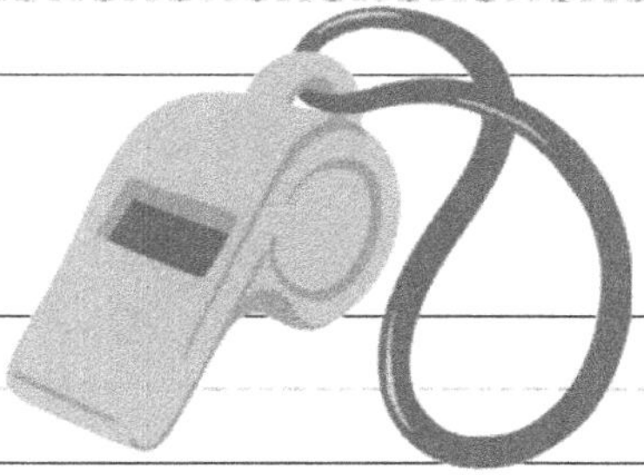

whistle

whistle

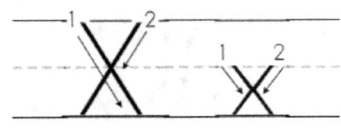

Trace the individual letters.
Then trace each toy name
and then say it aloud.

X X X X X X X X

X

X X X X X X X X

X

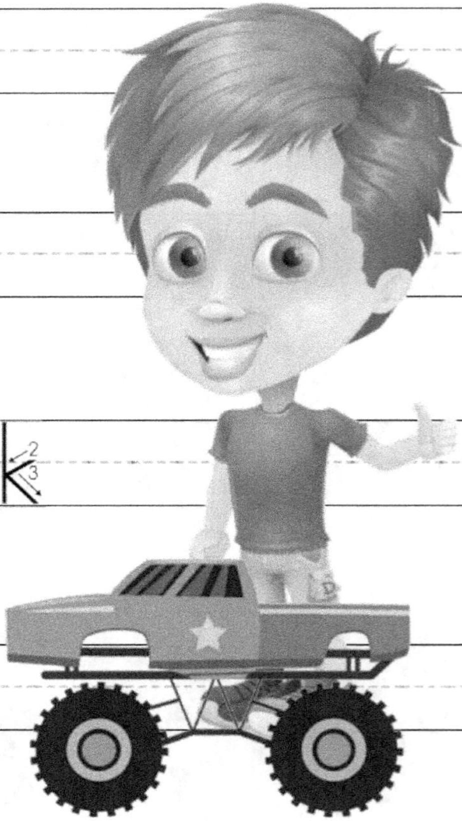

XL Truck

XL Truck

XL Truck

WRITING WITH THE DANGER TWINS

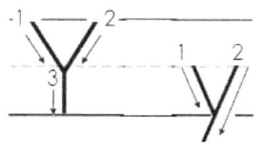

Trace the individual letters. Then trace each toy name and then say it aloud.

Y Y Y Y Y Y Y

Y

y y y y y y y

y

yarn

yarn

yarn

WRITING WITH THE DANGER TWINS

Zz

Trace the individual letters. Then trace each toy name and then say it aloud.

Z

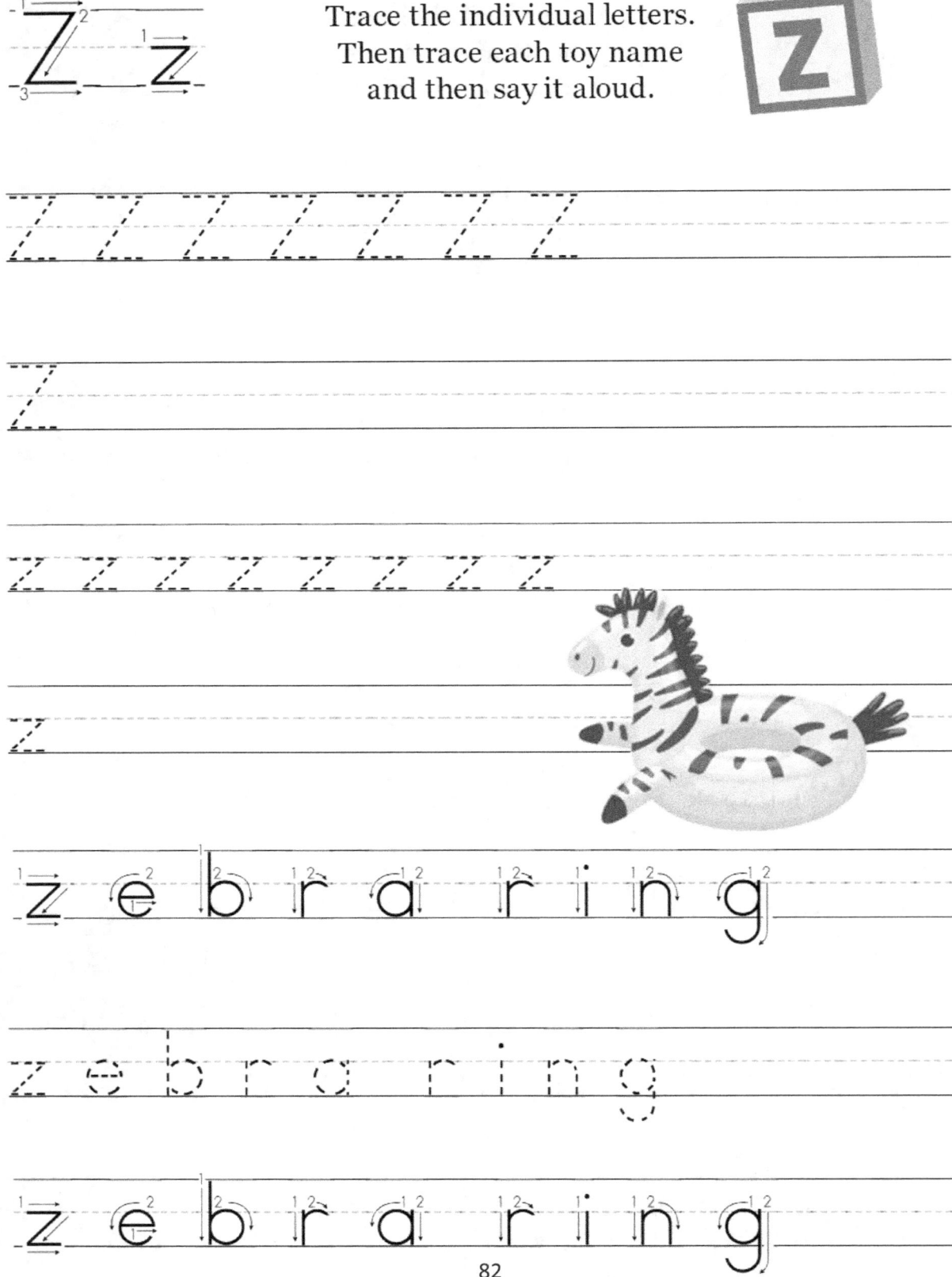

ZZZZZZZ

Z

ZZZZZZZ

z

zebra ring

zebra ring

zebra ring

The Danger Twins listed
their favorite toys.
Write your favorite toys from
the third section of this book.

slide   engine

letters top

theDangerTwins.com